REAL

SELF DEFENCE

GEOFF THOMPSON 4th DAN

JOINT CHIEF INSTRUCTOR C.E.K.A.

JOINT CHIEF INSTRUCTOR
THE BRITISH COMBAT ASSOCIATION

ABOUT THE AUTHOR

Geoff Thompson was a doorman for 9 years and has been a practising martial artist for over 20. He presently holds a 4th Dan C.E.K.A., 4th Dan B.C.A., 2nd Dan K.U.G.B., 1st Dan Modga Kung Fu and A.B.A. Ass. Boxing Coach. Geoff is a former British Weapons Champion and has also trained widely in Aikido, Judo and is qualified to teach Ju-Jitsu.

Geoff's first book, Watch My Back - A Bouncer's Story, is fast becoming a cult book. His second book, The Pavement Arena, has also been hugely successful. He now writes regular columns for Combat and Traditional Karate Magazines and Muscle Mag. He is fast becoming recognised as an international authority on the art of self protection.

His books on the art of punching and grappling will be released soon, also Bouncer, the sequel to Watch My Back.

ACKNOWLEDGEMENTS

To Gus and Tracy for their valued friendship.

Dennis Clinch, for all his help with my research on the law.

Brian Berry, for all his help with my research on the law.

Sharon, for all her backing.

Paul Clifton, without his help I would still be walking blindly along the literary path.

Mick Finnie, my old friend, for his help with research.

John 'Awesome' Anderson for showing me how to adapt.

Alan Peasland, for his help with the typing.

Les Jones for his valued friendship.

To Jacinta, a beautiful person. Thanks for all the hard work she put into the final type.

Paul and Bev Carpenter, for being there when I needed them.

To Simon and Edgi' from the Princes' Trust, thanks for all your encouragement.

For Sharon, as always, with all my love.

Also by the same author -

Watch My Back - *A Bouncer's Story*

The Pavement Arena - *Adapting combat martial arts to the street*

Summersdale Publishers
PO Box 49
Chichester
West Sussex
PO19 4LF
United Kingdom

A CIP catalogue record for this book is available from the British Library.

Printed and bound in Great Britain by The Book Factory, London.

ISBN 1 873475 16 0

I would like to dedicate this book to my late friend
Karen Jones
who was a great inspiration to me and to many others.
She was probably the fittest person I have ever had
the pleasure of sharing quality time with.
Also to Martin, Les and all the family
by whom she will be sadly missed.

CONTENTS

PROLOGUE

Throughout this text you will find a myriad of techniques that will cover you for almost every conceivable angle of attack. Before you engage and gorge the theories and tactics I endorse, please bear in mind now, that I always, always recommend 'flight' above 'fight'.

To engage in a physical confrontation when there is a chance of escaping is foolhardy and potentially fatal.

Violence may vary from 'fisty cuffs' to 'gun play', and from continent to continent the theories herein do not, they are universal. Fear control and the psyche are relative to most human beings and do not change with the country or climate.

Nearly all potential confrontations are avoidable if you follow the prescribed rules and use your common sense. Most of those that are not, if dealt with positively, are controllable. For the minority that are out of the purlieus of your control you will, no doubt, have to fight for your life, every scrap of knowledge you can pick up from this book, other books and actual self-defence classes will undoubtedly help to weigh the odds in your favour, even against the strongest of attackers.

Recent surveys have shown that capitulating to an assailant, or plea bargaining, "Do what you want, but please don't hurt me", (especially in rape scenarios) will and does not guarantee your safety. After all, is this person (attacker) before you the type you can trust to keep a deal? Capitulating victims also, in most cases, suffer far more than other victims with negative emotional aftermath, and anyway, why the hell should you 'give in' to these depraved individuals? "FIGHT BACK!"

Every confrontational situation is different in one way or another, for this reason I have listed, in the forthcoming chapters, physical (and mental) techniques for use as attacking tools. No matter what your size or stature, there will be something there to suit you, the ones that do not, discard them and pay added attention to those that do. Engineer and build them until they are second nature, then they will work for you.

Fear control? You may not discard this baby. This is the foundation upon which self-defence is built. No matter how hard or demanding you find the prescribed exercises, don't give in, stick with them. "If you are prepared to stand the heat of the forge you can mould yourself into whatever person you so desire. A weak person can become strong, a soft person hard."

It would be very easy for me to fill this book with a myriad of 'quick fix' pictures and illustrations and try to baffle you with photographic hogwash, after all, many others before me have done so, but that wouldn't help you. Why? Because 'real' self-defence is not about photographs or illustrations, although, as is perfunctory with books of this genre there will, when necessary, be the obligatory few.

I would preferably like to take the reader on a more realistic journey, one that takes you through the pit-holed, hurdled forest of self-defence so that when you arrive (safely, I hope) at the other end of the metaphoric forest and turn the last page of this illuminating text, you will be better prepared for it.

In an age where assaults upon the person are more common than fish and chips, where rape, robbery and murder are no longer 'shocking' because of their regular column in the pages of society, and where every journey from the home is a potentially hazardous one, (even the home is no longer a sanctuary from such assaults), self-defence can no longer be just a popular pastime, it should be an imperative part of our every day lives.

The information herein is derived from a lifetimes empirical survey where mental self-dissection, (very painful), was necessary to root out all of my own weaknesses before I could gain promotion and elevation to the highest plains of understanding and survival. Now, after many dangerous years of search and research, spending thousands of nights standing on cold night club doors and tangling with life's gratuitously, violent minority, I stand on the plateau of understanding, enlightened. Shocked beyond measure, but enlightened. I have studied the psyche of violent people first-hand, talked (and fought) with hundreds of professional street fighters, muggers and robbers, etc at times dropping (or rising, depending upon your views) to their violent primaeval levels. Now I pull away from the criminally obese, I draw my conclusions upon them and upon violence. From my conclusions is born a better understanding of how to counter such people in the face of a violent or potentially violent situation.

My conclusion? Fight fire with fire. To beat these people you have to be these people, at least for the few seconds/minutes it takes to neutralise them. The following chapters will tell you how. Please do not be disappointed when you discover that the defence tactics that I endorse are very basic and/or very grotesque, this is not a Kung-Fu movie, this is life and it is real.

This text will tell you how it is, not how I think it is or even how I think you want it to be. It is everything, like or hate, that you need to know. I have not been over-concerned about illustrating every conceivable way that you are likely to be attacked, that would be impractical and almost impossible. What I have been more concerned with is the victims state of mind before, during and after these attacks and how to overcome and control these states of mind so as to put you in a better defensive position.

A fire prevention video teaches you how to avoid a fire and how to cope in the unfortunate event of a fire, it doesn't try and make you into a fireman, and so it is with self defence. Awareness and avoidance are the most important facets, the physical techniques are merely a back-up system for when you fail to follow the rules.

For a greater insight into grappling and punching please refer to my books, *Real Grappling for the Street Scenario* and *Real Punching for the Street Scenario*.

INTRODUCTION

To find a book about Real Self Defence is a rare event for me. The emphasis is on real. Over the years I have seen a succession of Self Defence books written by people whose only experience of violent conflict has patently been in the arena of their own safe imagination. They write, evidently, from a perspective of never having been there themselves and garnish unreal scenarios with unworkable physical techniques.

Good Self Defence is first and foremost about avoiding violent situations, but should the worst arise it is equally about coping with instant fear and shock. The best techniques in the world are of little value if a victim, through fear, is frozen into immobility. A writer on Self Defence who is unable to portray these feelings and emotions so as to imbue in people a true sense about what conflict will do to them on an emotional level has not been there and his teachings are, as a consequence, meaningless.

Geoff Thompson does not fall into this category. Having successfully survived hundreds of violent confrontations in the front line of security work he knows and conveys these emotions in print to allow you the reader to experience safely the reality of violent conflict. The physical teachings, whilst important, are secondary. In this book you will read about Fear Control, Adrenalin Switches and the Psychology of Conflict. You will read about Awareness and Avoidance of Threat and, uniquely, you will read interviews with muggers to hear how they ply their trade of violence. From the other side of the coin there are interviews with the victims of such violence, but most importantly you will be hearing from a man who has not only been there, but who can portray with honesty the whole range of fear and emotions that need to be kept in control to survive confrontations.

Don't expect a magic photo sequence of techniques which you can adopt as the grail of Self Defence, expect to find the harsh reality of violence and how to keep control of one's self and emotions to be able to function on a physical level.

I commend this book to anyone who is genuinely concerned about their own Self Protection.

Peter Consterdine
7th Dan Karate ex Great Britain and England Karate International
Joint Chief Instructor British Combat Association (the principle British Self Defence Organisation)
Professional Bodyguard and Security Advisor.

FOREWORD

Whenever I hear the words 'self defence' my alarm bells start ringing and I think back to the Bruce Lee era when there were so many unqualified, so-called Martial Artists opening bogus clubs all over the country. ''Come and do a six week course and learn to defend yourself.''

The realities, of course, are very different. How very refreshing it was to receive such a realistic and effective approach to self defence written by Geoff Thompson, a Shotokan Karate third dan. His first hand experiences in working at night clubs have enabled him to adapt his Karate skills to more realistic self defence situations.

His philosophy is that if you can walk away from a situation you should do so, but if you are cornered you should be prepared, in all aspects, to defend yourself and being prepared is being well-practised!

This book will give you every aspect of self defence that you will need, what you have to do now is put them into practise. This is the best self defence book that I have ever read and I am sure that it will be a great help to you in the future.

Neil Adams MBE
Former World Judo Champion and Olympic Silver Medalist

CHAPTER 1

PREPAREDNESS

"Learn from nature: how often do you see the mouse playing by the hawk's nest?"
Sensei Harry Cook.

It is a well-known and well documented fact that most attacks upon the person, be it rape or robbery, are largely avoidable. It is not so well-known, though well documented, that the greater percentage of attacks upon the person, especially rape, are committed by the opportunist criminal, who will only commit the offence if it drops into his lap and he deems it a 'safe bet'. The 'safe bet' circumstances that spur on the opportunist attacker are the very same circumstances that you should avoid if you want to minimise your chances of being attacked. With unsolicited assaults you must use your common-sense to avoid the obvious scenarios and get it into your head that it can and will happen to you if you do not take precautionary steps.

Here are a few basic rules to follow:

1 AVOID areas/night clubs/pubs etc that you know have a reputation for trouble. To frequent these places is to court trouble.

2 NEVER take the short cut home if doing so involves going into or through sparsely populated or badly lighted areas. These places are notorious for harbouring the criminal fraternity.

3 ALWAYS keep in company whenever possible, you are far less likely to be attacked whilst with a group of people. Attackers mostly prey on the lone victim.

4 WHEN you have to walk alone down a dark or sparsely populated street stick to the edge of the path away from secluded doorways and entries. These are also favourite harbourings for attackers.

5 IF you are confronted never fight when you can run.

6 KERB CRAWLERS generally beckon their intended victims to the car, never move near to the car, be curt and do not engage in any conversation with anyone in the car.

7 FACE THE TRAFFIC when walking, whenever possible. If a driver tries to pick you up or force you into their car you will be running away from the direction in which he is heading. If you do find yourself in this situation make your way, quickly to the nearest lighted or inhabited area, also, try to get onto the opposite side of the street. This will make it increasingly harder for the attacker should he contemplate trying again. Don't change routes if doing so is placing you in a more vulnerable position or area.

8 PARKING LOTS/AREAS should be avoided where and whenever possible, if not they should be treated with great caution.

9 NEVER EXCEPT A LIFT from a stranger, your vulnerability is greatly heightened when you do so.

10 EMPTY HOUSE when you are returning to an empty house look for signs of forced entry, if you notice any, do not go into the house, get away quickly and quietly, phone the Police.

On the subject of rape it is said that most rapists are known to their victims before the assault, so take care. The psychotic stalking rapist so often portrayed in books, films and in the media are, thankfully, in the minority. In reality the rapist is likely to be someone that you know, though not necessarily well, who probably seems the last person on earth who would commit such a sick and depraved crime. So ladies, you need to be extra vigilant. All of the foregoing scenarios should be avoided and adhered to as a matter of course. In addition, and for basic avoidance and survival, be very fussy and sceptical about who you take lifts with or invite into your home. Until you know the person who wants to take you out etc, a little better, stick to places that you know well, better still try to go out in a foursome.

Any attempt at rape, whether thwarted or not, should be reported to the Police. Many, many rapists are free and walking the streets today because their victims were either too scared or too embarrassed to report the attack to the Police, often even too scared/ashamed to tell their own families of the atrocity. This reticence is understandable, but, every time a victim fails to report a rape or attempted rape, somebody else gets attacked or raped as a direct consequence because this sick individual is still at liberty.

CHAPTER 2

COMMON ATTACK SCENARIOS

"Knowing the place and the time of the coming battle, we may concentrate from the greatest distances in order to fight."
Sun Tzu.

If you know why, where and how an attack is likely to happen it stands to reason that the acquired knowledge will help you to avoid such situations, or prepare for them.

In bygone years, most, in fact nearly all attacks upon the person were relegated to the hours of darkness and the deepest crevices of seclusion, i.e. down a dark alley at night. So, hypothetically, if you avoided dark secluded places you were deemed as 'pretty damned safe'. Not so in todays liberated society where the said antagonists have crawled from out of the crevices, come off the night shift (although most do still favour darkness and seclusion) and anybody, anytime, any place are 'fair game'. Why? There could be a myriad of reasons. My own theory is that the judicial system that we follow in this country is laughable in its tolerance for the criminal ilk. Basically, the criminals know that even if they do get caught their sentence (if indeed they get one) will be a lenient slap on the wrist, in metaphoric terms.

The reasons 'why?' are not really important in the realms of this text because politics will confuse rather the enlighten the situation, what does matter and what you do need to know is how to stop the attackers and attacks.

There are, of course, lots of different types of attackers and attacks. Some choose to rob, some choose to rape, whilst others just love to instigate gratuitous violence on innocent people. (Some people like to combine all three). Some attackers are cold-blooded in that they meticulously plan their attacks before they set about executing them, most are 'opportunists' who will commit an offence if a 'safe' situation arises in their every day lives. All are uniform in two things. Their attacks are unsolicited. They have absolutely no regard for human life. It has been known for people facing a potential attacker to talk their way out of the on-coming attack, but as admirable as they may be they are few and far between. Men, women and children are being attacked absolutely indiscriminately often even in highly populated areas where the frightened and seemingly unsympathetic general public hide under the veil of, 'It's nothing to do with me', or 'I don't want to get involved'. So if you do find yourself in a dangerous 'attack' situation, don't rely on any help from the 'caring' passers-by, because more often than not that is exactly what they will do, pass you by. The attacker is generally a cowardly person who either fights from the podium of alcohol/drugs or attacks you from behind, possibly with the crutch of a weapon or an accomplice/s. Excepting possibly the rapist who works on the basis that he believes himself physically superior to his victim, most attackers work with the aid of one or more accomplices. Alone or with a team, these people, due to their proverbial 'yellow' streaks, will if you fight back ferociously with well aimed economical attacks, usually 'run'. (If they are not already unconscious).

One area that seems to be ignored in most self-defence books, shows and videos is what I refer to as 'talking distance'. Almost all attacks upon the person, with exception to the blind side attack where the attacker strikes you from behind, are preceded by dialogue. It may be aggressive, 'What are you looking at?', or it may be disarming, 'Have you got a light please?'. It could also be incidental, 'Haven't we met somewhere before?'. The attacker will say anything to gain and distract your attention before his attack.

The aggressive approach will be followed by an attack either before, during or immediately after your reply, as will the disarming and incidental approach. Their (the attackers) tactic is basic and effective. Engage the victims brain with a statement or question, when the brain engages it and is thinking of a reply, 'BANG' they strike with unexpected ferocity. So attacks are either instigated whilst the victim is not looking or not thinking, in the latter case, mind occupying dialogue is nearly always employed by the attacker prior to his attack. In a later chapter I will tell you how to use this approach to your own advantage.

Understanding the mechanics of an attacker can be a great advantage, after all, 'fore warned is fore armed'.

If you are approached by someone that you are not too familiar with, even if the approach turns out to be genuine and not a ploy, and he proffers a question or statement, courteously engage and answer the question, but at the same time prepare yourself both mentally and physically for the assault that will quite often ensue, by placing yourself, inconspicuously, into a small 45 degree stance (see illustration) as you answer. If the inquiry or statement is a genuine one then nothing is lost. If it turns out to be an 'engaging' ploy, you may from your pre-cocked position, launch a pre-emptive attack just as your assailant is about to launch his attack, thus beating him at his own game. It's called 'attacking the attacker'. After all the best means of defence is attack (I call it the Belgrano syndrome!).

Throughout this text you will notice a distinct lack of blocking techniques, in over 300 successful encounters I have never blocked an attack. When talking distance is running low and I am sure that an attack upon my person is imminent I will attack first and will not stop attacking until I can run or my attacker is incapable of any further assault upon me. Brutal? Overkill? Not really, if you're not doing it to them, they'll be doing it to you.

There is a school of thought that believes 'fighting back' will only antagonise your assailant more, thus increasing the ferocity of this attack. From my experience I have found that this is not the case.

Surveys throughout the world have also shown that attack and rape victims who 'fought back' did not sustain any greater injury than those who didn't fight back. It is also a well-known medical fact that rape victims who fight back against their attackers recover from the mental torture that often follows such an assault, far quicker than those that do not. The duration of most attacks is short, the longer the attack lasts the more danger the attacker finds himself in. This is another good reason why a counter attack on the part of the victim is essential, it complicates matters for the attacker who can ill afford the time delay that your reticence would cause. The more ferocious your 'fight back' the more likely he is to abort the assault. The archetypal attacker thrives upon the capitulating victim who is moulded into supplication by sheer fright. 'Fight back' will also draw attention from passers-by, another dangerous complication for the attacker that will, again force him to abort. SO FIGHT BACK.

In my research for this book I have interviewed many attackers and victims of attack, this chapter is based on those interviews and my own personal beliefs.

CHAPTER 3

FEAR CONTROL

"When the common soldiers are too strong and their officers too weak, the result is insubordination."
Sun Tzu.

"Fear is the friend of exceptional people."
Cus D'Amato (Mike Tyson's late trainer).

If your body is a gun, your hands and feet the bullets, then your mind is the trigger. Absence of the trigger renders the rest of the gun ineffective. Many people practice technique after technique in their bid to become physically competent. They become bag punchers and mirror watchers, convinced in their own minds that they can 'handle themselves', standing high and aloof on sugar pedestals and wearing their embryonic confidence like a thorny crown. When the rain comes down in the guise of an attack or confrontation their pedestals are melted and they crash to the cruel, cold floor of defeat and degradation with a resounding 'Bump'. All the time that they were developing 'Power' on the bag and building a sinewy, beach physique in the gym, they ignored the most important factor, the mental physique. This is, of course, not to detract from the physical training formerly mentioned, it is very important. Not though, nearly as important as the old, grey matter that will vehicle you, if properly trained, safely through the adrenalin build-up, the stress and pain of a physical encounter and the ever present aftermath that will all crush you flatter than a shadow if you do not or cannot control them, when they (completely uninvited) arrive.

If you know that these feelings are going to 'join you' their impetus is greatly lost. The shock factor of adrenalin can be scarifying if you do not understand or expect it, it renders many people 'frozen' in the face of an ensuing attack. What is it? What is fear? How can one define it? The dictionary informs us that fear is; 'an unpleasant, often strong emotion caused by anticipation or awareness of danger'. Cus D'Amato once said that, "the feeling of fear is as natural as the feeling of hunger or thirst, and should be treated as such". When you are hungry you eat, when you are thirsty you drink, you do not panic when you feel these pangs, because you know that they are natural feelings, so it should be with the feeling of fear. Don't panic, harness and utilise the feeling, fine tune it into a laser line of ferocious aggression that can be turned on and of with pin-point accuracy, missiled into your aggressors with devastating explosiveness.

Through my own searching and experimenting I have learned that the explosion inside the stomach that so many people struggle with and that causes the infamous 'freeze' syndrome which begets defeat is the adrenalin build-up. In primeaval days when men, (and women, when they weren't being dragged around by the hair), had to fight pre-historic animals to live and eat, the feeling of fear was an every day occurrence that did feel as natural and as common as eating or drinking. In todays society, which is very tame by comparison, the adrenalin release is no longer needed in our every day lives, in fact some people go through their whole lives without ever experiencing it fully, so when a situation arises that causes the adrenalin to flow and it arrives in one's stomach like a barbed bowling ball, and because we are so unfamiliar with it (unlike our pre-historic ancestors) we, naturally, neither welcome, use or like it (we panic). Psychologists call it the 'Fight or Flight' syndrome. In moments of danger the body releases a chemical, (adrenalin) from the adrenal gland that hits and goes through the blood-stream like a speeding tube train, preparing the body for 'fight or flight', deeming it stronger, faster and partially (sometimes completely) anaesthetised to pain. The more dangerous the situation the bigger the build-up and adrenalin release, the bigger the release the better you perform (run, fight), but by the same count, the bigger the build-up and release, the harder it is to control (bottle out, freeze).

THE A & O THEORY OF FEAR CONTROL

As I mentioned before, recognising the feeling of fear and understanding it does help to minimise the shock impetus. The question still left unanswered is 'How does one control the feeling once it is there?' By ignoring it. The feeling enters your stomach at a rate of knots and races around like a fly trapped in an empty jam jar. Your legs will probably start to shake (pre-fight shakes), your mouth will become dry and pasty, your voice will acquire a nervous quiver and you will probably experience tunnel vision. Ignore these feelings, they are all part and parcel of the adrenalin build-up and, though unpleasant, quite natural. The feelings do tend to lessen in intensity as you become more exposed to them. The aim is to master fear so that it becomes a fast moving vehicle with you at the steering wheel.

My own theory (The A & O Theory) of fear control, derived from facing violence as a way of life in society's culture dish, the night club, consists of giving adrenalin the run of your body until you are ready to channel it, a little like drinking water that flows around a tank until you release it with the turn of a tap. As a young Karateka I was, unfortunately, at the mercy of my own adrenal gland, when the adrenalin flowed, I ran. I made the classic mistake of thinking that the adrenalin flow was fear and that I was a coward, I also felt that I was the only person in the world who felt this way. Mike Tyson's analogy was that a coward and a hero both felt the same feelings in the face of adversity, the only difference being that the hero controlled those feelings and the coward didn't.

A & O? Accept and override. Accept fear into your body and then override it and get on with the job in hand. The ugly hand maiden of the adrenalin flow is the omniscient Mr Negative, that little man who perches on the shoulder of your minds eyes and tells you that you're frightened, scared or that you 'can't handle it' (the situation). Left to its own devices the mind can be a self-detonating time bomb of negativeness that will spiral you down into ever increasing misery. There are two ways of dealing with this tactician of corrosiveness (Mr Negative).

One, is to completely ignore him, not listening to anything that he says, thus leaving him no mental ledge on which to perch.

Two, counter every 'negative' with a 'positive' (this is the method that I practice).

"You're scared".

"No, I'm not scared".

"You can't handle this situation".

"Yes, I can handle this situation, I can handle anything".

And so on, and so on. By doing this you can erase the negative thoughts with the positive. It's very important that you do this because each negative thought that penetrates your psyche may and usually does erode a small part of your 'will' until eventually it (and you) is defeated, because negative begets negative begets defeat. So when the ship of your moral fibre is under the threat of mutiny from the minority 'yellow' crew within you, crack the whip of self-control and herd the craven back to captivity.

Once you have come to terms with Mr Negative and have learned to accept fear as a friend, override it and get on with the job of defending yourself.

Our own mind is used to being in control, if it says, "Stop", we generally do just that, if it says, "Don't fight back, you'll get hurt", (Mr Negative) generally we do not fight back and usually get hurt anyway. This is the body's automatic 'cut out' point, built-in by nature to protect the body and mind from 'burn out'. Due to evolution (and a distinct lack of pre-historic animals in our every day lives) and soft living this automatic 'cut out' is set at a very low toleration point, the slightest hint of stress or pain and the brain 'cuts out', leaving us well short of our desired goal and getting us 'beat up' by adversaries because we capitulate far too readily. This 'cut out' point can and has to be extended if we want to attain any measure of success in our self-defence. (Everybody's 'cut out' point is set at a different tolerance, some people are gifted with a very high tolerance rate).

Further into the chapter we will talk about how to extend it.

Just past the 'cut out' point, for those who dare defy the mind by going past it, is the infamous 'pain barrier' that even fewer venture through. Extending or erasing the 'cut out' point is the pot of gold at the end of the metaphoric rainbow, that will not be acquired without an epic and arduous battle with your own mind, but, if you can defeat yourself you can do anything. You must 'dare' yourself to take the challenge. Remember the old addage of the S.A.S., 'Who dares Wins'.

In brief; when you feel fear, recognise it for what it is, adrenalin, accept its presence calmly without panic, counter any negative thoughts and override them by getting on with the job in hand. This whole process, elongated here for the sake of description, usually has to be controlled in a matter of milliseconds, so practice is of the essence. It is very difficult to practice something that is not, or at least doesn't appear to be present in our every day lives. For the practising martial artist this task is not such a difficult one because he can, if he wishes, generate fear in himself by facing the top dogs from his or other Dojo (training hall) in sparring or partner work. This alone will spark the infamous adrenal gland, forcing himself to 'handle it'. As unpleasant as this may seem it's the only way.

To learn how to handle the heat you must force yourself to 'stay' and endure it. In addition, this practice will also help to extend the 'cut out' point and instil within you that all important characteristic which is pivotal in self-defence, self-discipline without which we would all be lost. Another great 'cut out' extender, whilst in the Dojo, is forced endurance. Force yourself through the 'pain barrier' by holding that stance a little longer, carrying on when every facet of your being is telling you to 'stop' and never giving into the elements of human emotion. Pain, fear, exhaustion, boredom and low esteem will all, at one time or another (sometimes they may all strike together) gnaw away at your weaker links trying to make you quit, give in, surrender or capitulate. Over coming and defeating these elements will greatly extend the 'cut out' point and help to develop a strong character. It is possible, eventually, to completely erase the 'cut out' point, where, in theory, you could go until you dropped. This, though, is singularly the most difficult goal ever to achieve, known as the illusive 'indomitable spirit'. The more that you experience and confront the 'fear' syndrome the more desensitised you will become to it and the easier it will be to control and thus harness the more that you 'confront and control' the stronger minded you will become. These exercises in 'confront and control' will build the mental muscle as a barr bell and weights will build physical muscle, the same dictum 'no pain, no gain' is also evident.

This gained strength of mind will put your whole life into perspective, all of a sudden those mundane tasks at work or around the home become a simple challenge by comparison, all are relegated to simple exercises in self-discipline, everything that life throws in your way become 'challenges' that you will no longer balk at, nothing seems beyond the purlieus of your mental capacity.

For the non-training person the task of generating fear, extending/ erasing the 'cut out' point and instilling self-discipline is not such an easy or obvious one. Joining a good martial arts club would be the easy and obvious solution. Unfortunately, not everyone has the time or the inclination to do this, so we need to look a little closer to home.

THE FEAR PYRAMID

To generate, and ultimately control fear (whenever I refer to fear, I refer to adrenalin and vice-versa) build yourself a fear pyramid. This can be a very private thing (it was with me). A lot of people will not wish to share their more private fears with other people, this reticence is understandable. It is imperative, though, that you do admit them, even if it is only to yourself, don't fob yourself off as I once did with feeble excuses like, ''I'm not scared of it (what ever 'it' may be), I just don't want to do it'', and other such inanities, after all an alcoholic cannot even begin treatment until he first admits to himself that he is an alcoholic.

That is the first and foremost step, one can go no further until this is complete, when it is list all your fears. Draw yourself a pyramid with as many, or as few, steps up to the pinnacle as you have fears, then fill each of those steps with one of your listed fears starting at the bottom of the pyramid with your least fear and finishing at the top step with your greatest fear. (See illustration). The common factor with all fears is that confronting them will cause an adrenal rush, it is 'confrontation' that sparks adrenalin, as opposed to the actual fear itself. For instance, a dentist's chair is frightening until you actually have to sit in it.

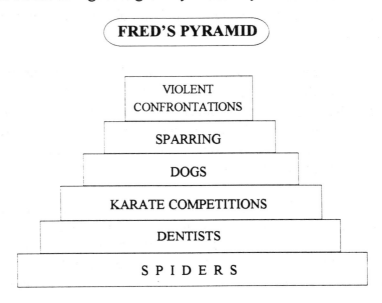

FRED'S PYRAMID

VIOLENT
CONFRONTATIONS

SPARRING

DOGS

KARATE COMPETITIONS

DENTISTS

S P I D E R S

This is a hypothetical example, 'Fred's pyramid'. Fred has filled his pyramid with all his own fears. He is scared of spiders, but of all his fears this one is his least, because it is his least fear and we do not want to try and walk before we can run, we will get Fred to confront this one first by finding a spider and picking it up, using the aforementioned A & O theory of fear control, Fred has to accept that he has a fear of the spider, counter any negative thoughts with positive ones then override the feeling by picking the spider up. It will not be easy so don't expect it to be, you may well spend half an hour in contemplation, it may even take you weeks or months to summon up the courage. Once Fred has managed to pick it up he should put it down and do it again and again until he no longer holds the fear. Once the fear is erased Fred would then progress to the second step on the pyramid and his second least fear, then repeat the process all the way up the pyramid until he reaches the peak. Sometimes one confrontation may be enough to deem you completely desensitised to the fear, other times you may have to repeat the confrontation several times. Fred may have to pick the spider up six times before he loses his fear of spiders, and yet only one visit to the dentist sees his fear of dentists decimated. The speed with which you travel through your pyramid of fears depends entirely upon yourself. It took me several years to get to the top of mine, though the time matters not, because with every fear you erase you will be gaining some degree, large or small, of gained mental strength, desensitisation, familiarity with fear and self-discipline. Every step you climb up the pyramid will make you increasingly stronger.

To many, picking up a spider that you hold a fear of or visiting the dentist when even the thought terrifies you may seem an eternity away from confronting and controlling a self-defence situation. I agree that they do seem poles apart, though, they are not, they are directly related because both scenarios require self-discipline and fear control, though, admittedly sometimes in different degrees. The importance of the former is that it actually builds self-discipline and develops a control over fear, which are both pivotal in the extension of the 'cut out' point. Also by confronting minor fears you are getting regular practice at the A & O theory of fear control. In theory, picking up a spider when you hold a fear for it, is the same as controlling the fear, so evident in a confrontational situation with an assailant, granted, they are at different ends of the 'fear' scale, but that is all the differentiates between them. As, and, if you go further up the pyramid that gap lessens more and more with every step. For instance, on Fred's pyramid, his fear of sparring and confrontational situations are separated by one step, and once he has confronted and erased his fear of sparring there is no longer a gap at all.

As a final note on fear control I must state that all the foregoing exercises will generate fear enabling you to practice control and gain desensitisation, the fear generated will not be as intense as the real thing, nothing can be. The new found enlightenment and self-discipline, though, will help you immeasurably and get you as close to the real thing as is humanly possible, so that when the real thing thrusts its self at you in the guise of a confrontational situation you will be prepared.

Conscientious practice of the foregoing theories have helped me to confront and master fears that I was under the dominion of for many years, and has made me a strong-minded person. As a young man I held a great fear of confrontational situations, with the aid of the A & O Theory of fear control I met my fears head on, spending 8 years working as a night club bouncer.

CHAPTER 4

ATTACKING TOOLS

"Security against defeat implies defensive tactics: ability to defeat the enemy means taking the offensive."
Sun Tzu.

Attacking tools, there are many, and different schools of thought adhere to and promote different tools. Some talk of the indomitable boxer, with fast, punishing 'hands', others about the cripple, shooting 'kicker' or mauling 'grappler'. In fairness every discipline has its strengths and its weaknesses, its good exponents and its poor ones. To be a good all-rounder you need a compilation of all the disciplines. You need to be able to wrestle, box and kick. For 'blood and snot' self-defence, economy of movement is the name of the game. Why risk a high kick, when a poke in the eye would suffice? Why spend ten seconds executing a complex set of movements, when the same result could be attained with a one second movement? I have been there and tried it all, what I am left with is a small nucleus, (very small), of techniques that have and will work in a live situation. This text will show you what I deem to be the most effective, also those that are less frequent, though still effective for the odd occasion, when the latter might be of use.

In this chapter I have listed the attacking tools without too much detail, that will be left to the specialist chapters where each individual 'tool' will be isolated and dissected.

HEAD:
Best when used inside punching and wrestling distance. May be used to butt from the right, the left, the front or to the rear, using the corner, front or rear of the head to attack. Also, effective if executed in an upward manner using the crown of the head to attack. Whilst grappling the cranium, hair may be rubbed into the opponent's eyes.

TEETH:
Only effective within wrestling distance to bite anything, especially protruding items of the anatomy; i.e. nose, ears, etc.. (false teeth may be thrown at an assailant).

MOUTH:
Spitting into an opponent's face or eyes can be a great distracting factor that may lead you onto a better grip, attack etc

SHOULDER:
Effective for close-in fighting if thrust into opponent's wind-pipe or face.

ELBOWS:
Effectively used from any angle whilst in close range.

HANDS:
May be used to punch in any direction with power. To pull and twist whilst in grappling distance, to palm, heel or to gouge with the fingers extended.

HIPS:
Pivotal when executing throwing techniques if thrust into opponent's mid-section, ensures depth and unbalances him before the throw.

KNEES:
May be used to thrust inward, upward and around to the body or the head or by dropping knee first onto the 'felled' opponent as a finishing technique.

SHINS:
May be used to attack any part of the opponent's anatomy, especially the knees and thighs.

FEET:
May be used to attack front, side, back or round ways to any part of the opponent's anatomy. Especially effective whilst attacking the oppo-

nent's lower regions. Lower abdominals, pubic bone, groin, knees and shins.

INCIDENTAL WEAPONS

''He who only sees the obvious wins his battles with difficulty, he who looks below the surface of things wins with ease.'' Sun Tzu.

Anything be it a hand-bag or a forlorn piece of brick on the floor may be employed as an 'incidental weapon'. Some will fall within the realms of the law, others outside it. All are uniform in one way, they are extensions of your hands. It is impossible to include every conceivable weapon within this text, because almost everything may be used as a weapon. I will try to cover the main weapons that you may carry on your person. The greatest draw-back of most 'incidental weapons' is availability. Most are concealed in pockets or bags, so are not readily available, at least not quickly enough, in the face of an ensuing attack. You can look pretty conspicuous walking down the street weilding a stick or bat. Something less conspicuous would be a rolled-up newspaper or an umbrella.

HAIRSPRAY/DEODORANT:
Great as a 'hit and run' implement. One spray in the eyes of an assailant would prove very painful, distracting him long enough for you to 'run'. They must, for obvious reasons, be aerosols. A sturdy aerosol cannister would also act as an effective 'bludgeoning' tool, if in close to your assailant.

UMBRELLA:
A sturdily built brolly could prove a very effective attacking tool for gouging into the eyes, throat or by swinging, base-ball-bat style, at the assailant's face. Lacks the solidity of a bat or stick.

HAND-BAG:
The classical 'joke' weapon, so often portrayed in comedy sketches. In reality the 'bag', if sturdily made with metal rims etc, can be used effectively as an attacking tool, (especially if you put a brick in the

bottom of it). Its greatest weakness lies in the fact that it must be swung to attack, deeming it 'telegraphed'. Can be a good defensive tool against a knife attacker, if used to 'parry' the blade.

PEPPER:
A small pot of pepper, with an easily detachable lid, is easy to carry/conceal and fairly inconspicuous. When thrown into an attackers eyes it becomes a fine 'hit and run' implement.

NEWSPAPER:
Famed by the great 'eye-spy' writers as a lethal weapon. Due to its celluloid fame, it is often looked upon as 'unrealistic'. If used correctly against the eyes or throat, it is indeed a deadly weapon. Its great beauty lies in its accessibility and inconspicuousness.

KUBOTAN AND KEYS:
A wonderful little weapon that is both effective and legal (indeed a rarity!), with multi-various facets. In the hands of an expert its uses are limitless. Used as a simple punching weight, or by attacking in a slashing motion, with the attached keys. The bottom of the kubotan barrel can be used to stab or gouge. The kubotan and keys may be combined to wrist lock or choke an assailant. (It has also been known to successfully hold one's keys.)

Kubotan & Keys

PEN/PENCIL:
Inconspicuous, accessible and potentially deadly, if aimed at the softer more vulnerable areas of the assailant's anatomy; i.e. eyes, cheeks, throat, etc

CREDIT CARD:
The fine razor edge of a credit card deems it a potential killer if purposely or inadvertently aimed at the jugular or other main veins. Very accessible, extremely legal. Would take a lot of practice to become proficient with this weapon.

For a more in-depth look at the legality of 'incidental weapons', please refer to Chapter 25 - 'The Law and Self-Defence'.

CHAPTER 5

AREAS OF ATTACK

"Emerge from the void, strike vulnerable points, shun places that are defended, attack in unexpected quarters."

Due to the anaesthetic qualities of adrenalin and the opponent's possibly/probably being under the influence of drink/drugs, pain per se is not usually enough to stop their attack. Most of the time they won't feel it. For this reason attacks should, in the case of body shots, be penetrative, striking the nervous system, or, in the case of head shots, accurate (jaw etc) so as to cause disorientation or unconsciousness.

In medical terms, every single part of the anatomy, if severely attacked, could potentially prove fatal. Even if the said blow was not a death dealing one, the accidental consequences of it may result in death. For instance, a blow to the nose may render an opponent unconscious, if in falling the relaxed head strikes the pavement or another hard surface, which from my experience it very often does, a serious concussion or skull fracture may occur, resulting in a possible brain clot or haemorrhage, ending in death. Death may also ensue, in this instance, due to the huge amount of blood from the nose clogging the throat during unconsciousness, which in turn stops the flow of oxygen to the brain, causing death. Even a kick to an opponent's shin, could in an extreme case, result in death, from shock or in the case of an 'arterial embolism', where-by the break splinters small particles of the decimated bone into the torn blood vessels, these abnormal particles become lodged in a vessel too small to permit their passage, which in turn may be identified as a blood clot from another part of the body, which could cause circulatory failure of a section of the body, causing gangrene and/or ultimately death.

In reality though, breaks, unconsciousness and death are not so common. The human body can be a very durable piece of machinery and not an easy vehicle to stop once it is charged with the pain reducing quality of adrenalin. As the potential victim in a self-defence scenario, one should never worry about the medical implications of your counter-attack/pre-emptive attack on the said antagonist, to do so would cause indecision on your part and indecision begets defeat, even a second of indecision can mean the difference between life and death, survival and destruction. The bottom line here is 'he' is trying, unsolicitously, to hurt/rob/rape you, to pay him any consideration would be foolhardy and dangerous.

Undoubtedly, the three most vulnerable areas of attack are the eyes, throat and jaw, though not necessarily in that order. Their vulnerableness lies largely on how they lie in relation to your attacking tools at the time of any particular altercation. You would, for instance, have little chance of attacking any of the three if you were grabbed from behind, for this reason, it is wise to learn other vulnerable areas so as to cover all situations.

HEAD:
Anywhere above the opponent's eye-line is a no-go area (unless you are using a weapon). To strike the skull with your fists or head is, mostly, futile. The cranium, being of thick and strong construction to protect the master muscle, the brain, does just that, though it is vulnerable to kicking techniques if your assailant is horizontal. The temple is, of course, very vulnerable, but it usually takes pin-point accuracy to be effective.

EARS:
Attacks to the ears, especially when both ears are attacked together, can be potentially fatal if unconsciousness and concussion occurs. If both are attacked simultaneously with cupped hands, rupture of the ear drum, via large amounts of air being forced into the internal canal of the ear, would ensue. In reality, this is unlikely to happen, though the pain inflicted by such an attack would likely be enough to stop your assailant long enough for you to make your getaway. The ears can also be ripped by gripping and pulling, though this can be difficult if the 'ear' is sweaty. The most effective attack against the ear is the 'bite' causing panic and extreme pain stopping even the most ardent attacker. A one-eared

assailant would also be very easy for the Police to trace, though I doubt they'd thank you for it.

EYES:

In my opinion the most vulnerable, accessible and sensitive part of the human anatomy. You may either scrape, poke or gouge them using the end/ends of the finger/s, depending upon how you are situated in relation to the eyes. Any connection between finger and eye will cause extreme pain and more often than not 'stop' your assailant, resulting possibly in a collapsed eye-ball, lacerated eye-lid or in some cases pushing the eye-ball completely out of its socket.

NOSE:

Because the nose protrudes from the face it becomes an obvious target, though not a favourite of mine. A strong aggressor would shake off such an attack and carry on. Because of its protrusion it is a very good target for biting. From a rear bear-hug the nose is a very vulnerable area for the rear head butt. As was formerly mentioned a severe attack to the nose could prove fatal, however, pain and watery eyes are far more usual.

THE JAW:

Most people who have experienced and participated in 'real' fighting with any degree of success will tell you that the jaw is the ultimate target for the ultimate fighter. Not because it causes pain or fractures, but because if struck correctly, it causes unconsciousness, which, in a defence or fight situation, is the ultimate goal, especially if you are facing more than one opponent. I will digress more in Chapter 18 - 'The Knock-out'. An accurate punch to the jaw bone will cause a shaking of the brain, which begets unconsciousness. Accuracy is of the essence if this is to occur. A severe 'knock-out' which sees the opponent unconscious before he falls can easily result in a fatality, if the head of the unconscious person strikes anything with a stronger construction than its self; i.e. the pavement.

THROAT:

Vulnerable is not a descriptive enough word to depict this accessible, susceptible area. Only partially protected by the jaw and neck muscles, and the fact that it takes accuracy to strike a telling blow. 'Chopping' and straight finger strikes are most effective when attacking the throat. A strong accurate attack may cause anyone of a myriad of contusions, from contusion of the internal jugular through to contusion of the Laryngenial nerve. A fracture of the Spinouse process to a possible injury to the Branchial Plexus, which would cause partial or complete paralysis of the arm. All the former ailments possibly resulting in death. For close in fighting, grabbing the wind-pipe around the Adam's apple sector and squeezing the Larynx tightly may cause choking, extreme pain and unconsciousness.

SOLAR PLEXUS:

Medically speaking, a severe attack to the Solar Plexus can cause anything from a deep fissure in the liver to a torn gall-bladder or even a complete rupture of the stomach, which may culminate in massive internal bleeding. Due to severe shock or blood loss this can end in death. More realistically you can expect to knock the wind out of your opponent, at the most, which would give you enough time to 'run'. From my own vast experience in these matters, body shots (unless employed as a finishing technique to a felled opponent) are 99% of the time, not 'stopping' techniques and should only be employed when there is no other option or target open to you. Adrenalin, with its pain reducing qualities, builds a brick wall around the body deeming it impervious to punches and kicks. You may even break ribs or cause internal damage to your foe and still not deter him at the time of his attack. As a paradox, an attack to the face/jaw will at the very least cause disorientation in your assailant, because of the simple fact that it 'shakes' the brain.

JOINTS:

All joints, finger, elbow, knee, etc are vulnerable to attack, but are largely well protected by surrounding muscle. Knees can be easily attacked with kicking techniques, if you are proficient enough with your feet to find the accuracy that is necessary to do so, paradoxically, it takes no skill at all to bend back an assailant's fingers.

GROIN:

Anywhere around the lower abdomen and pubic bone area is very vulnerable to knee, foot or fist attacks. A severe attack to these regions may rupture the urinary bladder causing shock, internal bleeding or thrombosis, even a clot in the Femorial vein, which could ultimately lodge in the lungs causing death. Again, though possible, these are unlikely in reality due to the aforementioned metaphoric 'brick wall' syndrome. If no other target is available to you though, this is still worth a try.

TESTICLES:

In my time I have kicked, punched and grabbed this supposed vulnerable area in a bid to 'stop' an attacker usually to no avail. My lack of success has been largely due to them being so well protected. Attempted infiltrations with foot and fist have been lost to either the assailants large front leg muscles that sentry the testicles or the assailants instinctive 'thrust back' action. In the case of the 'grab and squeeze' the assailants underpants and trousers demand an iron grip to get even a whimper. Paradoxically, if you are fortunate enough to score a direct hit, that is an entirely different manner.

These, to my mind, are the major attack areas of the human anatomy. As you can see I am not a great believer in 'body shots' for the aforementioned reasons. Whilst you have a choice, always attack the eyes, throat or jaw, if these areas are not available for attack, aim for the most vulnerable area that is. Never expend energy on non-vulnerable areas like the skull, back, chest and shoulders. Whilst some of these areas do conceal major organs that may be susceptible to attack they are too well protected by major muscle groups to penetrate.

You may only have one shot so don't waste it.

CHAPTER 6

THE PSYCHE

"A whole army may be robbed of its spirit, a commander-in-chief may be robbed of his presence of mind."
Sun Tzu.

Adrenalin Switches

The following are all ways of operating your opponent's adrenalin, switching it off, begetting over-confidence by feigning submissiveness or switching it on to fool the opponent's reasoning process into believing they are scared (psyche out) by being or feigning fearlessness.

For every fight that I have witnessed or have been involved in where a physical response was employed, there have been another three where victory was gained over an adversary with guile as opposed to force, attacking the mind rather than the body. All that is involved is a little 'acting'. There are two roles you can play. That of a fearless fighter who will balk at nothing or no-one and is not at all frightened of the adversary before him, or the 'mad man' approach, aiming to instil fear into your potential assailant by becoming loud, aggressive and challenging. After all 'when ignorance is mutual, confidence is King'. Your ploy, in both cases, will be to frighten the adversary, via your portrayal, into aborting his attack attempt by making him think that you are something you're not. The common street term for this process is 'Psyching out'. Generally, this is acquired by throwing a challenge or accepting a challenge (to fight) without demur.

Here is a more detailed explanation of both roles:

1. As the cool unperturbed veteran fighter who is completely unruffled by the threat of violence and willing to fight at the drop of a hat, who would, in the face of a challenge from a gratuitously violent antagonist

who picks a fight for no other reason than 'he wants a fight', pre-empt his challenge, or expected challenge by challenging him.

''Hey, there's no use arguing, if you want to fight let's just do it.''

Or by accepting his proffered challenge.

''Yea, sure I'll fight you, no problem.''

This cool 'Devil-may-care' attitude suggests to the antagonist you are, because of your blatant disconcern, a veteran fighter who has trod this path many times before. More often than not this approach will 'psyche' the antagonist out and 'stop' his intended onslaught. Not many people will enter into a confrontation if they think there is a chance of them getting hurt.

2. You could go for the 'mad man' approach, which in my opinion is the more effective of the two. Again you will be accepting or issuing a challenge, but this time you will do so, not with a cool disdain, but with vehement 'mad man' aggression.

''COME ON THEN, I'LL FIGHT YOU! COME ON!'' When accepting a challenge, or;

''IF YOU'VE GOT A PROBLEM WITH ME, SHUT YOUR MOUTH AND LET'S FIGHT!''

When issuing a challenge, perhaps dropping the odd 'expletive' in here and there for authenticity. This approach leaves even the strongest of antagonist with mouths agape rendering them, most often 'bottleless'. Whether you opt for the 'cool' approach or the 'mad man' approach, it is always wise to 'line-up' the antagonist (details of the 'line-up' in the next chapter) in preparation for a pre-emptive attack or defence, just in case the 'psyche out' is not effective. If you have issued or accepted the challenge and the antagonist is in a state of hesitation, re-iterate the challenge before he has time to analyse and re-gather his dissipated 'bottle'.

The 'KIAA' spirit shout, (a loud shout employed by Karate practitioners to reinforce technique and spirit), is also very effective for psyching out a 'would be' attacker. I watched a man, stood between three other men who were about to attack him, raise his fists in what resembled a Karate guard and scream loudly with 'KIAA', the three men, obviously assuming that he was an expert, collectively lost their 'bottle' and ran for it. It turned out that the 'Karate man' had never done a days formal Karate training in his life, but he could 'scream' loudly. The American Red Indians used a similar principle of war cries and war paint to instil fear into their enemies before battle, with great effect.

All of these tactics are an attempt at switching your opponent's adrenalin on and instilling the infamous 'freeze' syndrome into them before they instigate their attack, making them believe that they have bitten off more than they can chew. You may also, if you wish, underline your resolve by slapping the potential antagonist across the face or pushing him as forcefully as possible backwards. This minimum physical contact (especially the 'push') greatly enhances the possibility of him 'freezing'. I teach these theories in my regular self-defence classes and they have, over the years, been successfully employed by absolute beginners. Even so, it is imperative that you prepare yourself immediately for its potential failure so that you will be ready for a physical response.

As a parallel you can attempt to disarm your opponent by switching his adrenalin off. The 'psyche out' is an attempt at playing the situation up to avoid a fight/confrontation by scaring the opponent. Its parallel, playing the situation down, is employed when you have decided that your only option is to fight. By being submissive and switching his adrenalin off you are merely priming him for your pre-emptive attack.

If you cannot get to grips with this the 'psyche out', for whatever reason, you may wish to adopt this approach and play the situation 'down' by feigning capitulation. Again acting is employed, this time, as I said, you are not trying to psyche the antagonist out, you are trying to relax and mentally disarm him in preparation for your pre-emptive strike. You do this by pretending that you are more scared than you really are, even to the extent that you tell them you are scared and don't want any trouble and ''Please don't hurt me''. The antagonist who will probably be as scared as you are will think that he has got you where he wants you. 'BANG!!' You hit him whilst he is mentally congratulating himself on an embryonic victory. This ploy is or can be devastatingly effective because the antagonist is so 'mentally disarmed' that your unexpected strike will have maximum effect. Because his body has prematurely dropped its defences, your strike goes through undetected and unopposed, leaving his body no time to prepare for its absorption, similar to the boxer who prepares himself for the punch that he sees coming, the impact of the punch is lessened due to the boxers prior preparedness. If the boxer doesn't see the punch coming and therefore cannot prepare for its absorption, 'BINGO', the boxer is knocked out. So it is with a stressful confrontation, the body prepares itself for the possibility of a physical blow, thus lessening its impetus. If you can convince the antagonist that you are going to capitulate and are, therefore, not a danger to him he will, consciously or sub-consciously, drop his mental guard. If you attack him at this moment of disarmament he will have no time to prepare and 'BINGO' your attack has maximum impetus and you have maximum results.

''Simulated disorder postulates perfect discipline; simulated fear postulates courage; simulated weakness postulates strength.''
Sun Tzu

CHAPTER 7

LINE-UPS

"Attack is the secret of defence: defence is the planning of an attack."
Sun Tzu

Most self-defence situations and attack scenarios, as mentioned in the foregoing chapters, issue rays of prior warning if you are perceptive enough to look for them. If you are foolhardy enough to heighten your vulnerability by placing yourself in a dangerous situation like walking down a dark alley at night etc, you cannot expect any prior warning and will have to make the best of a bad situation.

In Chapter 2 - 'Common Attack Scenarios', I talked about the verbal communication that nearly always precedes an attack upon the person and the victim who is quite often disarmed or shocked rigid by it, deeming themselves veritable punch bags for their attackers, because the verbal approach that is designed to 'disarm' and 'freeze' does just that, blinding the victim to the ensuing attack. The time lapse between the disarming, or scarifying verbal (which can be pitilessly short) and the attack is 'your time', the time for you to seize the moment, as it were, and pre-emptively 'attack the attacker' or elongate the verbal by replying to the aforementioned dialogue and turning the scales upon him by attacking his psyche with aggressive counter verbal, or even by mentally disarming him with capitulating dialogue as outlined in the previous chapter on the psyche. These seconds before battle are absolutely pivotal, they must be managed quickly and without demur, remember, hesitance begets defeat.

THE DISARMING APPROACH: would go something like this:

A man approaches you, his left-hand extended holding an unlighted cigarette.

**Asking for a light, directions etc,
often used as a ploy to disarm a potential victim.**

"Excuse me mate, have you got a light, please?" he asks, innocently.

"No, sorry, I don't smoke," you reply courteously.

'BANG!' he bludgeons you with his fist or weapon as/after you reply, then robs/rapes you as you lay in a semi-conscious stupor.

I will use the same scenario to demonstrate how you can use the 'time lapse' between talk and fight to defend yourself.

A man approaches you, his left-hand extended holding an unlighted cigarette.

"Excuse me mate, have you got a light, please?" he asks, innocently.

You move your right leg slightly behind you to form a small 45 degree stance (see illustration) and splaying your arms as though in exclamation, at the same time you reply courteously.

"No, sorry, I don't smoke."

'Bang', you bludgeon him with a pre-emptive strike just as he initiates his attack towards you.

If his request for a 'light' is a genuine one and he doesn't try to attack you then, obviously there is no need for your pre-emptive attack, in either instance you are prepared, and that is the most important thing. So essentially the 'line-up' is preparing oneself, mentally and physically, to strike first in the face of an ensuing attack. What you use as an attacking tool in the 'line-up' is your personal choice, out of necessity it is best to employ your strongest, most comfortable attack. I always use right-handed punches missiled from the back of a left-lead stance, this ensures the utilisation of all my body weight. Some may prefer to attack left-handed, the important factor is that your initial attack, whatever it is, is your best one, there is nothing to gain and everything to lose if you throw anything less.

Here are a few of the more common 'line-up' techniques:

RIGHT CROSS/HOOK:

Thrown from the rear of a left-leading stance can be devastatingly powerful and effective. Its only real infirmity is, because it is thrown from the rear leg, it can be slightly telegraphed. From a right-lead stance this technique may be executed using the left-hand.

Line up, lead hand controlling.

Right cross.

LEFT HOOK:

Thrown from the front leg of a left-lead stance. If employed by a 'practised' pugilist, this punch can be very destructive. Because it is thrown from the front leg it is less telegraphed than other techniques and it has less distance to travel to the target. Because of the high skill factor involved it is not a recommended punch for the novice.

Line up for left hook.

Left hook. Note the extreme hip commitment.

HEAD BUTT:

A very 'pain inflicting' attack, usually directed at the opponent's nose. If executed correctly utilising the body weight it can cause enormous damage to an adversary, though it is not known as a knock-out technique.

Head Butt from line up.

You may, if you wish, line-up an opponent with anything from a straight finger attack to the eyes, to a low side kick to the shin as long as you deem the 'employed' technique as an effective one in the circumstances. Always try to launch the chosen attack from a small 45 degree stance. This will enable you to maximise body weight transference and ensure your own balance and stability when you thrown it.

Never experiment with silly, flashy techniques for the sake of dramatic effect, be basic and ferocious, how it looks is not a factor that should even be contemplated. Many veteran fighters will survive hundreds of confrontations using only one technique, usually a right-hook or cross, pre-emptively attacking on the majority of those occasions.

IN SUMMARY:
Once you have lined-up the antagonist with your chosen technique (this should be done within the first second of any confrontation) and you are sure that an attack upon your person is imminent, distract and engage his brain with a conundrum, logical or illogical, it matters not as long as it engages his brain, then pre-emptively strike from your pre-cocked 'line-up' position. What you say to your antagonist is not important, what is important is that it veils the attack that you are about to employ. I have tried many variations, here are a few:

"Look, I don't want any trouble with you", 'BANG'.

"What are you picking on me for?" 'BANG'.

"I don't want any trouble, here, have my money", 'BANG'.

Questions, ie, 'Do you want my money?' are more effective at engaging the brain than a statement, ie, 'I don't want trouble', because a question demands an answer which will need thinking about. Even something completely abstract will cause engagement, ie, 'How did the City get on today?' because of the confusion factor, after all, what has the 'City result' got to do with the situation in hand? It is at this moment of engagement/confusion that you attack for the opponent will be 'blind' during engagement.

If the antagonist proffers a question you may wish your pre-emptive 'blurb' to be in the guise of an answer to it, or you may wish to feign deafness by saying, ''Sorry mate, I didn't here what you said'', preceded by your attack, if the situation calls for it. One thing is certain, the longer you take to strike, the more grave the situation becomes, for you, especially if you are faced with more than one antagonist, so you must 'act' as quickly as possible, hit and run.

Some attackers use the same, 'light please',or, 'time please', approach formerly mentioned and follow their verbal introduction with the threat of violence (usually backed by a weapon) as opposed to 'actual' violence. With these types, use the same tactic of 'line-up' and refuse their demands vehemently, shout loudly to attract attention and complicate matters for them as much as possible, this will cause them to abort their attempt. If not and they move closer to you, employ your pre-emptive strike and then run. Remember, most antagonists who only threaten violence do so because they do not want to use violence and will flee if you complicate the issue. (See Chapter 22 - 'Case Histories': The Attackers).

CHAPTER 8

HANDS AND ELBOWS

In my opinion there are no better instruments to employ as attacking tools than the hands, whether punching, poking or grabbing. The hands are to self-defence what Nureyev is to ballet. Elbows are also a valuable asset, though more of a rainy day technique than the irreplaceable hands, which are the most natural and accessible tools for 'defence' on the human anatomy.

The knuckles are, when the fist is clenched, an extremely solid and durable element, when abetted by the transferred body weight they become devastatingly destructive as an attacking tool. The fact that our hands are endowed with the sense of touch also aids the accuracy of an employed technique infinitely.

There are many ways in which one may practice and polish 'hand' techniques, some of which I will explore in this chapter. The bias will, understandably, lean toward methods that I favour. Some of the techniques and methods of practice may seem a little basic for the advanced or practising martial artist who, unrealistically, sees 'complex' as synonymous with effective. In real terms 'complex' is synonymous only with unpractical. To be effective the chosen self-defence technique must be economical and what is economical if it is not 'basic'. Paradoxically, the beginner will find no problem in practising the prescribed techniques, because of their fundamental qualities.

My advice to the novice who has no formal 'fighting' background is to chose his strongest side (right-hand if you are right-handed, left if you are left-handed) and practice one or two techniques, preferably a right-cross or a right-hook (see illustration). Make them, via conscientious practice, your own. Practice until you develop power and accuracy, then, especially if you employ the technique as a pre-emptive attack, you will have a good chance of defending yourself successfully.

My advice to the advanced or practising martial artist is exactly the same as that which I offer to the novice, choose your strongest technique and make it stronger, work it until it is absolutely natural and comfortable, of course, you should still practice all your other techniques and perhaps add to your 'specialist' punches as they improve.

In your bid to attain 'good hands' you will be looking to develop accuracy, speed and power, accuracy rising slightly above the other two necessaries, because speed and power are not, in normal circumstances, enough to knock-out an adversary without accuracy, by the same count a certain amount of speed and power are needed to companion 'accuracy' if it is to secure unconsciousness in an adversary. Later in the chapter I will go into depth about the development of the three foregoing elements. Firstly, I would like to look at the different attacks available via the 'hands'.

LEFT JAB/Finger strike/Claw:
As a punch the jab is generally used as an 'opener', a lead punch that lacks real power. Very good for causing irritation in an opponent through the stinging pain inflicted. Presence of the former and latter also help to make openings for the 'bigger' punches that you might wish to follow with.

Left jab with fist.

Jab with fingers.   **Jab with clawhand.**

The same attack used with 'open hand' transforms an irritating technique into a 'stopping' technique. This may be attained by either 'clawing' the hand or by coupling the fingers together to form a point then directed at the eyes. One of the most basic, effective and accessible techniques on the curriculum.

LEFT HOOK/Palm heel:

Thrown (as a right-handed person) off the leading left leg and aimed, ultimately, at the opponent's jaw. Very powerful if abetted by the transferred body weight. All hooking punches are thrown in the same style as a 'slap' attacking with knuckles as opposed to the flat of the hand.

Left hook with palm heel of the hand.

For maximum power push your right hip forward and slightly to the left before the strike. As you throw the left fist toward the target, pull the hip back to its original position and push your left hip sharply across and to the right, following the path of your punch. This hip movement will ensure maximum weight transference into the punch.

With the palm heel the foregoing criteria is the same using the heel of the hand to attack as opposed to the fist.

LEFT UPPERCUT/Palm heel:
Thrown from the leading left leg and aimed, ultimately, at the jaw. Very powerful if correctly employed. For maximum power push your right hip forward and to the left before you strike, slightly bending at the knees so that you are just below the target (jaw). Throw your left fist upward, twisting the fist on impact with the jaw, so that the palm is facing inward (to your own body), simultaneously, retract the right hip sharply to its original position and push upward from your crouched position, thrust the left hip forward and upward, following the path of the punch. On connection with the jaw, follow through with the punch and hip for maximum effect.

Left uppercut.

With the palm heel the foregoing criteria is the same using the heel of the hand to attack as opposed to the fist.

RIGHT CROSS/Finger strike/Claw/Palm heel:

A most powerful technique utilising (if correctly executed) nearly all of the body weight. Thrown from the back, right leg whilst in a left- leading stance. Throw the right fist toward the target (jaw), simultaneously, thrusting your right hip forward and in the same direction as the punch. Your hip should fully thrust in conjunction with the punches connection of the jaw.

**Right cross. Be sure to push your
body weight behind the punch.**

With the finger strike, claw and palm heel to attack as opposed to the fist. With the finger strike and claw the target area would be the eyes as opposed to the jaw.

RIGHT HOOK/Palm heel:

A powerful, accessible and natural punch. Applied with the facsimile of a 'slap' using the knuckles as opposed to the flat of the hand to attack.

Right hook.

Thrown from the back, right leg whilst in a left leading stance. Throw from the outside-in, in a semi-circular motion toward the target (jaw). Throw the fist toward the target, simultaneously, thrust the right hip sharply forward, following the route of the punch. As it connects with the jaw follow through with the punch and the hip for maximum power. With the palm heel the foregoing criteria is the same using the heel of the hand to attack as opposed to the fist.

RIGHT UPPERCUT/Palm heel:

Thrown from the back, right leg whilst in a left leading stance. Bend slightly at the knees so that you are just below the target (jaw). Throw you right fist upward, twisting the fist on impact with the jaw, so that the palm is facing inward (toward your own body), simultaneously, push upward from your crouched position and sharply thrust your right hip forward and upward following the path of the punch. On connection with the jaw follow through with the punch and hip for maximum effect. With the palm heel the foregoing criteria is the same using the heel of the hand to attack as opposed to the fist.

Right uppercut.

ELBOWS

The elbows are almost as versatile as the hands, though employed, usually from a shorter range. Because of their close proximity to the body they are, potentially, more powerful than the hands, however, they lack the 'feel', accuracy and cunning of the 'hands'. They may be used off the front leg or rear to uppercut, thrust (sideways) severe strikes or (whilst in grappling range) as a downward strike (see illustration).

For hooking and uppercutting with the elbow, from front or rear, the foregoing criteria in the section on hook and uppercut punches is the same, using the point of the elbow as opposed to the fist to attack.

DOWNWARD STRIKE: (against a waist or leg grab)
Lift your right (or left) arm up high with the palm of your hand facing away from you. Pull it down in a rapid descent aiming the point of the elbow at and into the target, (spine, neck, rib cage).

Downward elbow strike.

SIDE THRUST: (against an assailant attacking from the side)
Bring your right (or left) arm across the front of your chest, palm
inwards, as far as it will go, then thrust back along the same route, aiming
the point of the elbow into the oncoming or stationary attacker. Target
the Solar Plexus, throat or face.

Side thrusting elbow strike.

REVERSE ELBOW STRIKE: (against an opponent at your rear) Stretch your right arm out in front of you. Turn you head and look at the target behind. Sharply retract your arm back from its out-stretched position and behind you, aiming the point of your elbow at and into the assailant, simultaneously, step back with your right leg to add weight to the attack. Target the Solar Plexus, throat or face.

Reverse elbow strike.

The elbows are just a shortened version of the 'hands', only use them as back-up to hand techniques or when it is not possible or practical to punch.

EQUIPMENT

FOCUS PADS: (Hooks and Jab Pads)
Potentate amongst training aids are the focus pads. Excellent for the development of accuracy, power, distancing and multi-angled punches.

Focus pads. Aim for the spot in the centre of the pads.

Each pad is centred by a one and a half inch (in diameter) 'spot', that acts as the target area. Anything but a direct hit on the 'spot' looks, feels and sounds wrong. An accurate shot will feel solid and emit a definite 'thwack', letting you know that you are on target. They are excellent for anyone wishing to develop a knock-out punch.

It is necessary to have a partner when practising 'the pads', he should fit one pad to each hand and then angle them to meet the demand of your desired punch. Spot facing inward for hook punches, downward for uppercuts and forward for straight punches. The person punching the pads should lead with his left leg (right if right-handed) and punch the pads with his left-hand, to his partners left side, and his right-hand to his partners right side. The 'puncher' should employ a guard in normal practice and no guard in 'line-up' practice. The holder should vary the height and distance of the pads (from the puncher). As the puncher hits the pads he should exhale through his mouth or nose, this will regulate the breathing, feed the working muscles with oxygen and aid 'Kime' (body focus), forcing ones muscles to tense on impact of the punch or strike.

Once the puncher becomes familiar with hitting the pads and the holder with holding them correctly, the 'holder' may dictate and control the play by shouting out strikes for the 'puncher' to execute.

"Jab, cross, right hook, left hook", etc, then change the angle of the pads to receive the designated strikes. The experienced puncher may attempt more advanced combinations, "left jab, right uppercut, left hook etc", again the 'holder' moves the pads in time with the strikes. The 'holder' should not stay in the same position all the time, he should move, forcing the 'puncher' to employ footwork. Each time the 'puncher' finishes his punch or combination the 'holder' should move to a different position.

When practising the 'line-up, pre-emptive strike', it is important to precede each strike with a disarming or engaging statement (as covered in Chapter 7 - 'Line-ups'). You must 'line-up', disarm/engage and then strike as though it were the real thing. Some people may feel a little foolish talking to an inanimate object (the pads) but realism is of the essence in practice, so I feel it is important to get as close to reality as is humanly possible.

TOP AND BOTTOM BALL:
Suspended in mid-air via a length of elastic from floor to ceiling, the top and bottom ball emerges as a wonderful piece of equipment, that is excellent for the development of timing and distancing. Some argue that it is the closest one can get to a 'live' opponent, I am not inclined to disagree. It is also a hugely enjoyable method of practice. May be used to practice jabs, crosses, hooks and to the advanced player; uppercuts. 'Line-ups' may also be worked on this versatile training aid.
The height (and thus the speed) of the ball can easily be altered by tightening the straps above and below the ball. In practice, if you stand

close to the ball it will, if you are not vigilant, hit you on its return or 'bounce' back, this adds to the realism of the practice immeasurably.

THE PUNCH BAG:

Probably the oldest method of practice known to the fighting man, despite its ancient heritage, it is still the very best power developing implement on the market. Also known to be excellent for developing good technique, stamina and combination punching. Also good for practising 'line-ups'. Because of the punch bags 'mass', accuracy development is not aided here, though everything else is.

If you dress the bag is a sack or even drape some old clothes around it, it becomes a fine implement for practising grabs and combinations of grabbing and striking.

SPEED BALL:

Set at a height just above your own head, the speed ball is, basically, only good for building the Deltoid muscles (shoulders), that are instrumental in the maintaining of a high guard. I do not see any other benefit to be had from practising on the speed ball.

The greatest form of practice, without a doubt, is to be had with a 'live' opponent/partner with whom you can communicate, learn and progress. Tell each other when a technique feels right, wrong, realistic, unrealistic, powerful or weak, etc If you do not, or cannot train with a partner, make your bag or pad work as realistic as possible using visualisation (see Chapter 20 - 'Visualisation'). Imagine the bag/ball/pads is/are real antagonists and that you are in a real situation, try to charge every blow to the foregoing implement with aggression, perhaps imagining that your life depends on the success of the said strike. This method of practice not only adds realism to the training session, it also makes the session therapeutic.

CHAPTER 9

LEGS

As attacking tools the feet are both powerful and accessible, though less immediate than the hands, and harder to master. Basic, low kicks are favourable if you choose to employ the legs as attacking tools.

Kicking techniques can be irreplaceably destructive, in theory. In practice 'live' situations lack the space and distancing to employ the 'kick' to its full potential, and just by the fact that you are using your legs as attacking tools renders you less mobile.

Great kickers (they are few) will doubtless disagree with me, and as exceptions to the rule, work effectively every kicking technique and theory that I would deem as ineffective. The techniques that I promote and practice are aimed at the greater majority who would or could never, even given the right distance, employ a successful kicking technique, and not at the smaller minority who could probably kick a cat out of a tree. To the minority I apologise profusely before I start, because I am sure you will not like what I have to say. Even the minority would, though, I'm sure, agree that when aiming at the masses one is obliged to promote techniques that will not take a life-time to learn. I can get a complete novice punching hard and accurate on the focus pads in one session, preparing them, in a small way, directly for the 'street', to do that with a kicking technique is a near impossibility.

Personally, I use kicks to 'bridge the gap (when the gap between you and your opponent is too great to employ punching techniques, you use the kick to 'bridge the gap'), or as a 'finishing tool' (to finish of a felled opponent). In the former and latter scenarios 'feet' are irreplaceable, especially the latter. As independent attacks, in most circumstances, I do not endorse them. I only kick if there is no other option open to me, though I always, without exception, 'finish off' with feet.

FRONT KICK:

Very basic and effective, especially when directed at the lower regions such as groin, knees and shins. Balance is not impaired (if kept low) and little skill is needed in execution.

Front kick. Lift the knee . . .

. . . and strike . . .

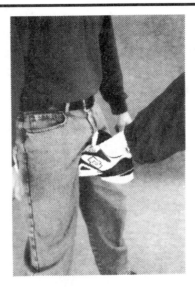

. . . using the in-step . . .

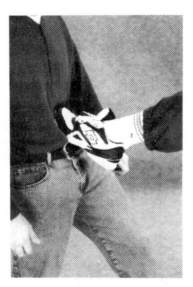

. . . or the ball of the foot

May be used as a thrusting kick attacking with the heel by pulling the rest of the foot back, as a snap kick attacking with the ball of the foot by pushing the ankle forward and pulling back the toes, or by attacking with the in-step by pushing the toes forward.

Any area below the waist is a safe and legitimate target, more specifically the groin, pubic bone, testicles, knee caps and shins.

The most important aspect of the front kick is the utilisation of the hips. Forward hip thrust is pivotal if any power is to be generated. A fast recovery of the spent kick is also imperative, (this applies with all kicks), a lazy kick will be grabbed by an adversary.

SIDE KICK:

Very powerful and accessible, though restricted by its high skill factor. May be executed to the front or the side attacking with the heel or the side edge of the foot by turning the attacking foot inward and pulling the toes back tightly so that the side of the foot is taut and prominent. If attacking to the side: Lift the knee of the attacking leg upward, thrust the foot sideways at the target whilst simultaneously pivoting on the supporting leg so that the foot of the supporting leg is pointing in the opposite direction to the target, this will ensure full hip commitment. After connection with the target recover the attacking leg quickly along the same route as it was aimed.

Face off, side kick, using the reverse leg.

Lift your right knee to the front . . .

and thrust leg forward, pivoting on the support leg to ensure hip commitment. Use the side of the foot or heel to strike.

Face off, side kick using lead leg.

Lift the lead knee high . . .

. . . and thrust heel or foot edge in the opponent.

ROUND-HOUSE KICK:

Very powerful and accessible, with a much higher skill factor than the front kick. Any target below the chest is a safe and legitimate one, more specifically the ribs, kidneys, lower abdomen, groin, pubic bone, testicles, thighs, knees and shins. The higher the target area aimed for with this kick the more danger there is of impaired balance and a slow recovery, unless you are highly skilled.

Face off for round house kick.

Lift the knee of the attacking leg (left or right) . . .

. . . and strike, pivoting on the support leg using in-step . . .

. . . or the ball of the foot.

The attacking part of the foot can be the in-step or the ball of the foot. If employing the ball of the foot pull back the toes and foot so that on impact with the target the heel is higher than the toes. If employing the in-step push the toes and ankle forward and strike with the bone at the front of the foot. It is important to lift the knee of the attacking leg high and to the side, throw the designated leg around and into the target by pivoting on the supporting leg and thrusting the hips behind the technique on impact with the target. After contact with the target quickly retract the leg by pivoting back on the supporting leg and pulling the hips back to their original position.

BACK KICK:

Potentially a very powerful kick. Accessible whilst attacking to the rear, a high skill factor if aimed at a forward facing opponent. The latter entails much skill and is, therefore, not recommended for the novice.

Face off. Back kick with turn. **Turn clockwise, lift attacking knee to your front, your back towards the opponent.**

Thrust attacking heel into opponent's body.

Using the heel of the foot to attack any of the lower anatomical regions, more specifically: Solar Plexus, ribs, groin, pubic bone, testicles, thighs and knees. Hours of practice is needed if accuracy is to be gained with this kick.

Attacking to the front: A potentially hazardous kick because it is necessary to turn your back, for a split second, on the opponent when twisting around, due to this 'twisting' action disorientation often occurs.

If using the right leg to attack, lead with the left leg. From this small compact stance lift your right leg up and toward your left leg wrapping the in-step of the right foot tightly around the back of the left calf muscle. Pivot around on the left supporting leg so that your back is directly facing your opponent, simultaneously turning your head so that you do not lose sight of him. Thrust the heel of the right foot, propelled by the forward thrust of both hips, into the target. After connection with the target, twist your body around and place the attacking (right) foot on the floor so that you are now facing the opponent.

Back kick to opponent behind you.
Lean away from opponent's grip.

Lift your attacking knee . . .

**. . . and thrust the heel into
the opponent's body.**

Attacking to the rear: Turn your head around so that you can see the target/opponent. Lift your right knee up to waist height and directly in front of you. Thrust the attacking heel directly behind you and into the target/opponent, propelled by the forward thrust of both hips following the route of the kick. After connection with the target retract the kick sharply back to the 'knee lift' position in front of you. Replace the foot on the floor. Alternatively, after connection with the target, twist and place the attacking foot on the floor so that you are now facing the opponent.

STAMPING KICK:

Simple, accessible and very destructive. Used mostly as a 'finishing' technique, but may also be used in vertical grappling as an ankle or foot 'stamp'. Effective on any part of the horizontal, human anatomy, more specifically the head, neck, ribs and legs.

Lift the knee of the attacking leg high and directly in front of you. Stamp the heel of the attacking foot into the target.

Lift your knee . . .

. . . and stamp with your heel.

SWEEPING KICK:

Used to 'sweep' an opponent's legs from under him. Devastating if followed up with a 'stamping' kick. May be used to attack and sweep the opponent's front leg, or both legs by attacking the opponent's rear leg.

Front leg sweep: Used to attack an opponent who has one leg leading (right or left). Attack the shin of the opponent's lead leg with the in-step of your right foot (left if attacking his left leg) sweeping his leg across the front of his own body spiralling him to the ground. Especially effective if the opponent is transferring weight onto the leg as you attack it, or if he already has weight on the leg.

Face off for front leg sweep.

Attack the opponent's front leg ankle with the inside of your foot (left or right).

Hook and sweep the opponent's leg away.

Back leg sweep: This attack relies heavily upon the opponent who is standing with his leg/feet close together. Attack with your strongest side, again using the in-step of the foot. Attack the back of the opponent's knees, lifting him completely off the ground, toppling him to the floor.

EQUIPMENT

All kicking techniques, for realism, are best practised on or with a 'live' partner. However, other implements may be used for the development of power, distancing and accuracy.

PUNCH BAGS:
Ideal for practising front kicks, round-house kicks, side kicks and back kicks. If you lie the bag flat on the floor it is also good for practising 'stamping' kicks.

When executing front kicks, side kicks and back kicks on the punch bag you may swing it, and kick it with the designated kick as it comes back toward you. This is excellent for practising distancing on a moving target. For low kicks and sweeps, a long 6ft bag that hovers just above the ground is recommended.

FOCUS PADS:
Specifically good for practising front snap kicks (using the in-step rather than the ball of the foot) and round-house kicks, will help to develop power, distancing and more importantly accuracy.

By holding one pad to the thigh, target area pointing outward it may be used to practice low round-house kicks. If tucked under the opposite armpit, target area pointing outward, ideal for mid-section round-house kicks. If held at groin level, with the target area pointing to the floor, may be used to practice low front snap kicks, using the in-step of the foot to attack. If held across and slightly in front of the body, target area pointing outward and at face height, may be used for 'face height' round-house kicks.

Focus pads or punch bags are good for practising kicks.

STRIKE SHIELD:

Excellent for developing power in all the kicks, because the shield is held along the contours of the 'holders' body, the practice has the added bonus of realism. If the holder tucks the shield tightly to the backs of the legs and bottom, the attacker may practice realistic low round-house kicks and sweeps.

CHAPTER 10

KNEES

Made famous by the ferocious Thai boxers who use the knees as naturally and as effectively as the western boxer uses his hands. Relegated to in-fighting or grappling though irreplaceable when applicable. May be used to attack upward, forward, round-ways or, to a felled opponent, as a finishing technique downward. Attacking as low as the opponent's knee or high as his head. Very basic and very accessible with, in some cases, a low skill factor.

UPWARD KNEE

To the groin or testicles this is a simple but effective technique. Lift the knee upward as sharply as possible. A slow push movement could/would be ineffective, the quicker the ascent, the greater the impact. If applying the same technique to the opponent's face or head, first grab his head by the hair or ears or by coupling the fingers of both hands at the back of his skull and pull his head down rapidly toward your knee. Simultaneously, bring the attacking knee upward to meet the descending head/face. As they meet, smash the head through the knee.

Grab the opponent's head . . .

and thrust the point of your knee upward into his face.

FORWARD KNEE

Much the same technique as the thrusting front kick using the knee as the attacking tool as opposed to the foot. Relies heavily on the grip you have on the opponent. Grab the opponent's attire tightly at about shoulder level and aggressively pull, via the said garment, the opponent's body quickly toward your knee. Simultaneously, thrust the attacking knee upward and forward to meet the opponent's body on its descent. At the moment of impact thrust both hips forward and into the opponent's body whilst still pulling downward with the grip.

Grab the opponent's attire . . .

and thrust your knee forward into his body.
Note the extreme hip thrust for power.

ROUND-HOUSE KNEE:

Much the same as the round-house kick, using the knee as the attacking tool as opposed to the foot. Also relegated to grappling distance and relying much on the pulling/grabbing support of your hands. May be used very effectively to attack the opponent's knee, thigh or body. The advanced exponent may even attack to the head.

If the opponent grabs your attire . . .

**Thrust your knee around ways
into the side of his thigh or body.**

To the knee, thigh or body lift the attacking knee up and slightly away from your body then thrust it downward toward the target and at the same time pulling the opponent via his attire toward the attacking knee. On impact thrust your hips forward and slightly drop your body weight into the technique.

KNEE DROP:

A very damaging technique to finish off an opponent who is already lying of the floor. Logically, the heavier you are the more effective this technique will be, although it doesn't rely entirely on body weight for its effectiveness. It can be dangerous for the person attempting the knee drop, because of the danger of being pulled into grappling range by the person on the floor.

Literally, you drop all of your weight forward and down onto the opponent, landing on the target area; ribs, head, etc, with the point of your attacking knee, (left or right). The quicker the descent, the more effective the technique. For added effect you may jump up so that you are landing on the opponent from a greater height.

Knee drop. Lift your knee high or even jump upward . . .

and land on the felled opponent with the point of your knee.

EQUIPMENT

PUNCH BAG:

The best way to practice knee attacks on the punch bag is to 'clothe it', either by tying a loose sack around it or dressing it in old clothes, so that you can grip it like you would a real opponent. Then grab and knee as you would a real person. As with kicking the bag, you may, if you wish, swing the bag and knee it as it swings toward you. If you lie the bag down on the floor you can practice the knee drop on it. A 6ft bag is great for practising lower region strikes.

FOCUS PADS:

Not as effective as the bag, but still quite good. The holder holds one pad tightly against his thigh with the target area pointing outward whilst at the same time thrusting his knee, (round-house), into the pad. To practice the upward knee, the holder should put both hands, (padded) in front of himself at about groin height, right hand overlapping left with both palms facing toward the floor. The attacker may take hold of the holders hands and pull them downward into the uprising knee or alternatively, grab his attire at shoulder level and pull on them as he executes the knee attack on the pads.

Practise the knee attacks on the pads.

CHAPTER 11

THE HEAD

One of the most effective techniques available if used correctly. If used incorrectly can be as dangerous to the bestower as to the recipient. The key factor in the success of the head butt is to keep the attack below the opponent's eye-line. Anywhere above the eye-line is potentially dangerous for he who delivers it. Paradoxically you, the person employing the 'butt' must use only that above the eye-line to attack with or again, you may get more damage than your opponent. You may attack with the head in five ways.

i) From right to left using the left corner of your forehead to attack.

ii) From left to right using the right corner of your forehead to attack.

iii) A forward thrusting butt using either the left, centre or right of your forehead to attack.

iv) You may attack upward with the crown of your head, or,

v) Backward with the back of your head.

They are all close range attacks that can be employed with or without the support of your hands to pull. Power in the butt relies on the combination of two things: The whiplash effect whereby you lurch the body forward slightly before the head, thus forcing the head to follow creating the whiplash effect, and the propelling body weight which should still be travelling forward as the head strikes its target thus adding weight to the said attack.

LEFT TO RIGHT:

Lurch your body forward followed by the head. The right corner of your forehead whiplashes into the right side or front of the recipients nose, face or jaw. If you are actually gripping the opponent's attire at the time of your attack, pull them via your grip, rapidly toward the head butt.

Face off for head butt.

Attack left to right.

RIGHT TO LEFT:

Lurch your body forward followed by the head. The left corner of your forehead whiplashes into the left side or front of the recipients nose, face or jaw. If you are actually gripping the opponent at the time of your attack, pull them, via your grip, rapidly toward the head butt.

Right to left.

FORWARD THRUSTING HEAD BUTT:

Lurch your body directly forward followed by the front of your head, whiplashing it into the opponent's nose, eyes or jaw. Care should be taken when attacking directly from the front not to hit the opponent's teeth. Although it is very painful for the recipient, it is also potentially dangerous, due to his teeth, to the attacker. If you are actually gripping the opponent's attire at the time of the head butt, pull them, via your grip, rapidly toward the attack.

Forward head butt.

UPWARD HEAD BUTT:

Generally employed from within grappling range when your forehead is in the region of your opponent's chest. From this position thrust upward rapidly attacking your opponent's chin with the front crown of your head.

Upward . . .   **and through.**

REVERSE HEAD BUTT:

To be executed when an opponent is standing directly behind you or is holding you in a rear bear-hug. In the case of the former, lurch your body rapidly backward followed by your head, whiplashing the back of your skull into the opponent's face. In the case of the latter where the body weight is locked in the bear-hug and, therefore, redundant, bring your head slightly forward then throw it backward as quickly as you can, hitting the opponent's face with the back of your skull.

Reverse. Lean slightly forward and . . .

thrust back into the opponent's nose.

EQUIPMENT

Basically, to practice the various head butts with any realism you need a partner. If this is impossible, (not everyone wants to be used for head butting practice!), then a punch bag will suffice. Treat the bag practice exactly the same as you would a person, standing yourself in the correct position in relation to the bag according to which 'butt' you want to practice. Beware, though, of prolonged practice and over zealous butting. It can cause extreme headaches.

CHAPTER 12

CHOKES AND HEADLOCKS

Employed only whilst in grappling range, though, devastatingly effective. A good headlock or choke, if employed correctly, is a definite
'stopping' technique, usually rendering your opponent unconscious.
Very accessible and not over complicated with a low skill factor. Some
are employed from the back and side whilst others are used direct from
the front. Some of the strangles use the opponent's jacket or shirt as an
aid and for leverage, whilst others (naked strangle locks), work
independently without the use of the opponent's clothing. Many may be
executed whilst in the vertical position, whilst others work more
efficiently in the horizontal, ground work position.

When familiarity with chokes and head locks is gained it is probable that
one may flow into another giving you a bastardised choke or headlock
of your own invention or design. This matters not as long as it 'stops'
your opponent. Basically, the function of the choke or headlock is to cut
off the blood supply to the opponent's brain, which in turn cuts off the
oxygen, via the side choke/headlock by compressing the jugular and
cartoid veins, thus stemming the flow of blood/oxygen to the brain. Or,
by directly cutting off the oxygen by compressing the wind-pipe, via the
choke. Either of the former or latter will bring unconsciousness within
seconds. All of the following chokes and locks can prove fatal so, in
practice, be careful.

REVERSE NAKED CHOKE:
Standing at the rear of your opponent, place your right arm around and
across his throat, clasp your right hand with your left and apply pressure
to the throat by pulling backward with the combined force of both hands.
It is important for maximum effect to make sure that the bony part of
the right wrist is against the throat as opposed to the softer forearm. It
is also beneficial if you can pull the opponent backward and off his feet,
this lessens his 'fight back' chances.

Reverse naked choke.

SLIDING REVERSE COLLAR LOCK:

Standing at the rear of your opponent, place your right arm around and across the opponent's throat and grip hold of his jacket or shirt. Place your left arm under your opponent's left armpit and seize his right lapel, (or jumper/shirt). Apply pressure by choking in a wringing action.

Sliding reverse collar lock.

SIDE HEAD LOCK:

Place your right arm, around your opponent's neck and hug his head tightly into the side of your own body. The palm of your right fist should also by facing inward so that the bony part of your right wrist is into the opponent's neck. Place your left palm heel underneath your right fist and apply pressure on the neck/jugular pushing up with the left hand and squeezing in with the right arm hand.

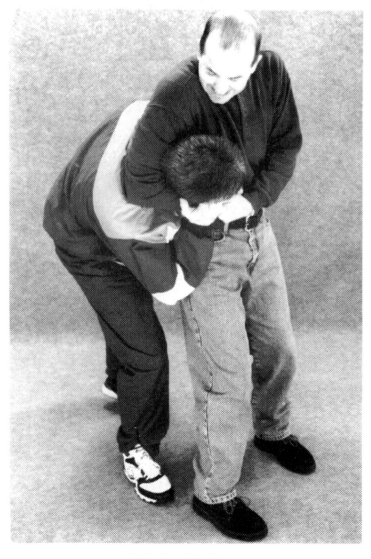

Side head lock.

UPPER THROAT LIFT:

Place your opponent's head under your right armpit and slide your right arm under and across his throat. Your right fist palm should be facing into your own body to ensure that the bony part of your wrist is along his throat. Place you left palm heel under the right fist. Apply pressure on the throat by pushing the right arm up and into the throat with the left hand whilst at the same time pulling the right arm into the throat.

Upper throat lift.

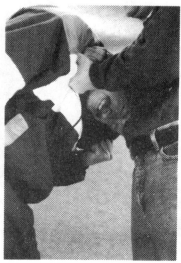

A close-up.

CLAW SQUEEZE AROUND THE LARYNX:

Simple and highly effective, especially if the opponent and yourself are grappling on the floor. Grip the larynx, which is situated at the top of the wind-pipe just below the chin and squeeze tightly.

Larynx grab.

SCISSOR CHOKE:

Whilst sitting on top of and astride your opponent cross your hands with palms down and grab the opponent's lapels as deeply to the back of the neck as possible. Apply pressure to his neck by pushing both elbows simultaneously downward forcing both wrists into either side of the opponent's neck.

Scissor choke.

SCARF HOLD AND FIST CHOKE

Sit at your opponent's right side and place your right arm around your partners neck taking a firm grip on the attire with your right hand. Wrap the opponent's left arm firmly around your own waist and hold his sleeve with your left hand. Clamp your left arm over your opponent's right arm firmly. Keep your right knee bent and close to your opponent's right shoulder and your left leg slightly behind you and straight. Now that the opponent is firmly held down make a fist with your left hand and push it hard into the right side of the opponent's throat.

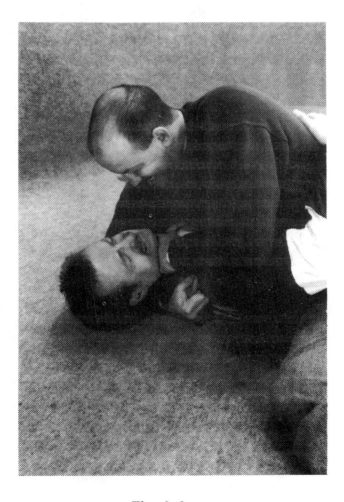

Fist choke.

EQUIPMENT

The only equipment available for the practice of chokes is the 'live' partner. Extreme care should be observed in all practice of chokes. The 'tap system' should be employed at all times and a choke should always be released immediately if the opponent 'taps'. There is no real set situation where you may use a choke or lock, it is just a case, when grappling, of remembering them and looking for appropriate openings.

THE TAP SYSTEM:

When a choke, lock or hold is 'on' the opponent taps the floor, himself, his partner or anything close enough to tap, to signal submission.

CHAPTER 13

THROWS

A good throw can be spectacular and effective (although it is only the latter that we are concerned with), and for the advanced Judoki or wrestler, very accessible. In reality their accessibility is dulled by the very high skill factor that is demanded in pursuit of competence. They are far more effective in my opinion if preceded by a strike, (head butt, bite, etc), as a feint. As a singular attack the 'throw' can quite easily be neutralised, even by a strong novice.. If, however, you bite the opponent or butt him before you throw, the success rate percentage of the throw elevates markedly.

Naturally a throw can only be employed realistically whilst in grappling range and it is fair to say that if you are in grappling range, generally, it is because of an error on your part. Grappling, especially to the non-grappler, is unique. It is the non-grapplers quick-sand because, unlike kicking and punching range which you may move in and out of at will, once your in it (grappling range) you will very rarely get out of it before the culmination of the fight. So it is best avoided. Being human, of course, we do make mistakes and to not prepare for such arisings would be both short-sighted and foolish.

There are a myriad of throws that basically fall into three categories: Foot throws, hip throws and shoulder throws, with a few others in between. The more complicated movements would be unapplicable, (to the beginner), in the street. The more basic the movement, the easier it would be to apply. As with punching and kicking combinations a bastardisation of the throwing techniques may be, accidentally or purposely, sought and executed and as long as it is effective then use it. The sacrifice throw, as taught in many grappling disciplines, whereby the thrower sacrifices his own safety in a last ditch attempt at throwing his opponent, is not a throw I would recommend in an attack situation.

You could well end up more damaged than the person you are trying to throw.

MAJOR OUTER REAPING:

From the grappling range this throw is both simple and highly effective, though relies, as do all throws, on a fast explosive attack.

Major outer reap.

Break opponent's balance.

Reap your attacking leg forward.

Then sweep the opponent's leg back . . .

. . . and throw to the ground.

Break the opponent's balance backward to the right corner as you simultaneously, advance your left foot forward. Continue to draw the opponent's balance outward as you reap your right leg to the back of the opponent's right leg throwing him backward. Try always to precede with a butt, bite or stamp to distract the opponent from the throw. To attack to the left side reverse the instructions.

HIP THROW:

Break the opponent's balance forward to the right front corner, as you simultaneously, advance your right foot toward the opponent's right foot. Make a body turning in entry and place your right arm around the opponent's waist (or neck). Make sure that both of your feet are inside the opponent's and your bottom is tightly into his groin and your knees are bent. Throw the opponent forward fast and explosively over your hip. May be reversed.

Hip throw.

**Break the opponent's balance as you
advance your right foot forward.**

Throw the opponent over your hip.

MAJOR INNER REAPING:

Break the opponent's balance backward as you simultaneously, reap your right leg through and around the opponent's lower leg, lifting the leg off the ground. Push the opponent (or butt him), violently backward. May be reversed.

Major inner reap.

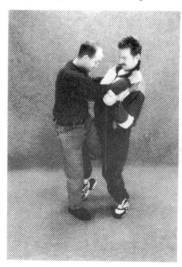

Break opponent's balance whilst reaping his leg.

Lifting his leg off the ground . . .

Push or butt the opponent backwards.

SHOULDER THROW:

May be used on an opponent who grabs from the back as well as the front.

Shoulder throw.

**Break the opponent's balance whilst turning in movement
and passing your right arm under the opponent's right arm.**

Throw the opponent over your right shoulder.

Break the opponent's balance forward as you, simultaneously, advance your right foot toward his right foot. Make a body turning in movement as you, simultaneously, pass your right arm under the opponent's right arm gripping hold of his attire. Try to keep both of your feet inside the opponent's and bend at the knees then throw the opponent over your right shoulder fast and explosively. May be reversed.

MINOR OUTER REAPING ANKLE THROW:
Break your opponent's balance to his right back corner, as you simultaneously advance your left foot forward and bring up your right foot. Reap the back of the opponent's right heel with your left foot. May be reversed.

SWEEPING ANKLE THROW:
Advance your right foot forward forcing your opponent backward on his left foot. Take a wide left step as you advance your right foot inward to support your body weight. Break the opponent's balance to the right side and simultaneously sweep his feet together as you lift him upward. Throw him with speed and force. May be reversed.

Sweeping ankle throw. Break the opponent's balance.

Sweep his feet together as you lift him upward . . .

. . . and throw.

BODY DROP:

Break the opponent's balance to his right front corner. Advance your right foot toward the opponent's right foot. Position your body so that your right foot blocks the opponent's right ankle and your left leg is bent. Throw the opponent directly forward and over the back of your right ankle with speed and force. May be reversed.

SWEEPING HIP THROW:

Break the opponent's balance to his right front corner and simultaneously advance your right foot toward the opponent's right foot. Continue to swing your body into position so that the left foot is positioned in the centre of gravity. Sweep the back of your right thigh against the front of the opponent's right thigh, continue sweeping your right thigh backward and throw the opponent directly forward and over your thigh. May be reversed.

Sweeping hip throw.

**Break the opponent's balance as you advance your
right foot towards the opponent's right foot.**

**Sweep the back of your right thigh against
the opponent's front right thigh.**

Throw the opponent directly forward and over your right thigh.

INNER THIGH THROW:

Break the opponent's balance forward to his right front corner. Advance your right foot toward the opponent's right foot. Make a body turning in movement so that the left foot is positioned in the centre of gravity. Sweep your right thigh upward on the inside of the opponent's right thigh, continue sweeping your right thigh up and back, throw the opponent directly forward and over your right thigh with force and speed. May be reversed.

Inner thigh throw.

Break the opponent's balance as you advance your right foot.

Sweep your right thigh up on the inside of your opponent's left thigh and throw with force.

All the throws may be executed from your right or left side depending upon which you favour and your position in relation to the opponent at the time of the throw. Of course, in theory, if at all possible you ideally want to throw the opponent clean and clear of yourself. In reality this is not usually the case. More often than not when you throw an opponent in the street situation, he maintains his grip upon you, even though he's been thrown, and pulls you down with him. The only solace one can extract from this fact is that you, the thrower, will usually end up in an enviable position of on top.

Don't expect an opponent to just 'let' you throw him, it can be a battle. Always try to distract the opponent with the aforementioned blow (butt, bite, etc), before attempting the throw for best results, and if he does maintain his grip after the throws and pulls you down with him, try to land upon him with the point of your knee, or elbow and break free at the first available moment.

A word of note, never deliberately seek grappling distance in order to execute a throw. Only attempt to throw if you find yourself trapped with no other options open to you. The element of surprise is pivotal in the execution of a throw, it must be fast and explosive, neither of the attributes will come without a lot of practice.

CHAPTER 14

GROUND WORK

Ground work is split into two categories. Grappling on the floor and fighting from the floor. The former is when you and your opponent both fall to the ground, the latter is when you fall, or are knocked to the floor and your opponent is still in the vertical position.

Both are very dangerous fighting areas to find yourself in, especially the latter. Some schools of thought advocate the latter as a first resort telling their practitioners to throw themselves to the floor before an attacker and fight from there. To me, this would be a last resort, (unless you are an extremely experienced ground fighter), and would be tantamount to throwing yourself at the mercy of an attacker. After all, isn't that (on the ground), where he wants you to be in the first place.

It would be easy, again, to theorise and show illustrations and demonstrations of how a felled person may attack and break an advancing assailants shin or knee-cap with a low line thrust kick or sweep him to the ground with a scissor throw. In reality, if you are on the ground and your attacker is standing, your chances, as a novice, of getting back up are minimal. Even an experienced fighter is facing defeat if he is on the ground. If both of you fall to the ground you have at least a 50% chance of winning. If you fall, or are knocked to the floor, your attacker will almost definitely go in for the kill, so it is imperative that you, the defender, quickly get yourself into a good defensive position. This may be lying on your side, left or right, where if you'll note both arms and legs are being used to provide support enabling quick movement and position change.

Positioned for defence.

Notice the knees and arms protect vital areas.

The right knee and right elbow are easily available to provide cover for the body, groin and head. From this position, hook one foot behind the attackers advancing foot to give you leverage, then thrust your right foot into and through his shin. Then get up before he can recover, or, kick out rapidly at the attackers groin or knees every time he approaches to attack. As soon as is possible, get up. Only attack or defend from the ground if you can't get back up. Never choose this ground fighting strategy, it's too dangerous.

Use hands and arms to absorb heavy blows.

Sitting up, the left leg and knee completely protect the groin and body whilst the left arm and elbow are ideally positioned to protect the head, it are also positioned well to block oncoming kicks. If the attacker attempts to punch your face, simultaneously parry the punch and kick the attackers left front leg with your left foot, trapping his leg in place. Grab the attacking arm at the wrist with your right hand whilst at the same time applying an elbow lock with your left hand. Twist the 'locked' arm in a circular motion and throwing the opponent to the ground. More simply and realistically, try to parry off the opponent's attacks until you can get up from the ground. The longer you stay down the less chance you have of getting back up again. If you find it impossible to get back up, try to catch hold of the attackers legs or arms and pull him down to the floor with you, where you have a more even chance. If you both fall to the floor it is important that you fight back hard and fiercely by striking the attacker in his vital areas, eyes, throat, groin, etc . . . Try to make the attacks calculated and accurate, don't waste time and energy on attacking the more muscular areas of the body. Bite, pinch, gouge, butt, knee, do anything and everything.

Attack the groin . . .

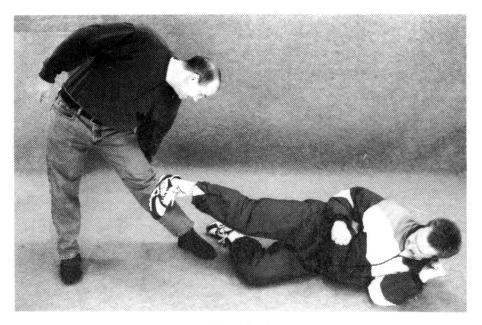

. . . or the shins/knees.

Remember, the attacker needs a quick result. He cannot afford to be rolling around the floor with you, scrapping it out. As soon as he realises that he's got a fight on his hands, the sooner he's going to want to get away. If you are severely pinned down and cannot move, feign supplication, pretend you've had enough and that you will let the attacker have whatever he wants. As soon as he releases his grip on you strike him hard in the eyes or throat with your fingers or fist, then run. Chokes and headlocks come into their own in ground work. All of the illustrated chokes and headlocks in Chapter 12, are hugely effective in ground work as are the eye gouges, head butts, bites, etc . . . These are a few illustrations of ground work techniques that I have successfully employed over the years.

The best way to practice these techniques is with a friend or your husband/wife or partner using the 'tap system' as a safety measure.

CHAPTER 15

BITING

A very unsavoury act (no pun intended). Barbaric some may say, and they would be right on both counts. One point outweighs both, it works. It is everyone's prerogative to omit or subtract to and from their fighting syllabus, whatever they so desire. Many find the thought of biting an adversary quite repugnant. However, when you're being attacked and your life is threatened, it loses it's repugnance, unsavouriness and barbaric tendencies at a rate of knots emerging from the cocoon of all three, as a life saving tactic in the savage 20th century. It has been my experience that when you bite an adversary, he capitulates readily, even if he doesn't, he'll remember you for the rest of his life.

There's not a great deal to be taught here that isn't already natural and obvious. For best results bit the protruding parts of the body. More specifically the nose, lips and ears, and if the opportunity arises, the male private parts. Don't make it obvious that you are going to bite or the attacker will easily avoid your attempt. Get as close to the target as possible, then attack fiercely and get as strong a bite and grip as possible. Whether you hold the grip or bite through and sever the target (ear, nose, etc), is entirely up to you and on the gravity of the situation. Be very wary of 'plea bargaining' attackers who will offer the earth to be freed from your bite. Their ploy is often to feign capitulation then, as soon as you release your bite/grip continue their attack upon you with added ferociousness. If you do decide to sway your bite/grip for freedom, make sure that you get to your feet (if you are not already there) before you release, then bite hard before you release, and run. This last infliction of pain upon your foe will give you valuable extra seconds to flee.

Here are a few illustrations of bites which I have successfully employed or have witnessed in 'live' situations.

Bite the nose . . .

. . . or ears.

I personally only 'bite' as a last resort, when all else has failed or is not available. Other fighters I know work the bite as a first resort attack whilst inside grappling range, even seeking grappling range to employ the bite. The former is my personal recommendation, though the choice is yours.

CHAPTER 16

DEFENCE AGAINST A WEAPON

The former scenario is getting more and more common place these days and attacks of these kind are always potentially fatal, especially with edged weapons such as knives. The first line of defence here is, always, avoidance. There is no facsimile to the movies where the attacker makes a deliberate strike with his attacking implement and you skillfully defend with a text-book block and counter attack. Attacks with a weapon are nearly always frenzied and multiple. To pick out one, of such a myriad, to grab or block is nearly always impossible, and so, impractical.

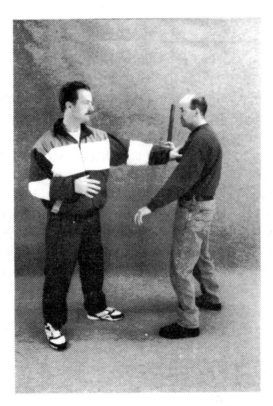

Keep the attacker at arm's length . . .

. . . and pre-emptively attack him.

In the instance of a knife wielding assailant, the most important thing to do is keep away from him, and, if there is a choice of avoiding the confrontation, do so at once. You should only fight an armed attacker if you are cornered and you have no other option. One mistake with a knife attacker could prove fatal to you. If you have an incidental weapon to hand such as a stick or a brick, etc.., which is unlikely, use it to attack the attacker or to knock the knife out of his hand. Kicking the 'knife hand' to disarm him can also be effective, though the skill factor of such a tactic is high. If you are carrying a hand-bag, use it to swing at the knife, or to parry a knife attack. If possible, wrap a coat or jumper around your leading arm for protection.

If the assailant does get to the stage where he starts to attack you, it will almost definitely be multiple attacks rather than the archetypal singular, telegraphed attack. Your best hope is to grab the attacking hand or wrist, being careful to avoid the blade, and attack the attacker with any means available to you, in the hope that he may drop the weapon. The photographs that compliment this chapter will demonstrate possible defences, but unfortunately, most defences against a knife (and most weapons), are highly skillful. Even a competent and practising martial artist must expect to get 'cut' in such an encounter.

Face off.

Kick the weapon out of the attacker's hand.

Long range kicking to the joints and quick, long finger jabs to the eyes are also worthy adversaries, but again, highly skillful.

**Use long range kicks to strike
the knifeman's joints (knees etc).**

Follow through with a knee strike . . .

Kick the weapon out of his hand.

If you have a 'spray' or there is grit on the floor around you, spray or scoop it into the opponent's eyes to give yourself time to escape. If an assailant has you pinned down with a knife or is holding it to your throat there is little you can do that will not directly endanger your life. The best solution in this case is to feign supplication and pretend to give the antagonist whatever it is he wants, until he is in a more favourable/ vulnerable position, then finger strike or punch fiercely at the eyes/ throat/jaw, in that order of priority, then escape. Remember, whether he wants to rob you or rape you, he nearly always has to remove the weapon from your throat, etc, at some stage, even if it is just for a second, covering the movement usually with a threat to hurt/kill you if you try anything. Especially in the case or rape/attempted rape, the threat of what he's going to do with the weapon is usually more predominant than the weapon itself. Recent surveys showed women who fought back against rapists came away from the scenario no more hurt than those who capitulated and did not fight back.

Wait for a vulnerable moment, if one is not, or does not seem imminent, manufacture one:

''Don't hurt me, just let me go while I get my wallet out and you can have it.'' Or whatever it is that the attacker wants.

Pretend to faint, or have a fit, this is something no attacker/rapist expects, in his confusion he may not see the attack you launch upon him.

In all of the formerly mentioned scenarios, make as much noise as possible to attract passers-by, draw as much attention to yourself as possible. This is a pet hate of attackers who will see it as an unwanted complication that may act as a catalyst in stopping his attack.

Practice using wooden or rubber knives as a facsimile to gain familiarity with a weapon wielding foe, remember though, when faced with a real knife in a 'live' situation it will feel and be a lot different, one wrong move and you may die.

Bars and bats are far more telegraphed than the edged weapon, though still highly dangerous. Having faced a few in my time, I can confirm that it is scarifying. Again, as with the knife attacker, try to keep out of the attackers distance. Because of the weight and size of such implements as bats and bars, etc, frenzied and multiple attacks are not so likely. Try to wait until the attacker swings with a wild attack, as the weapon passes you on it's forward thrust or as it is being retracted, rush in at the attacker and strike at a vulnerable area such as the eyes or knees/shins, then make your get away whilst he is recovering.

The accompanying photographs are my suggested defences against the formerly mentioned weapons. Never face an armed assailant whilst you have the choice of running away.

CHAPTER 17

DEFENCE AGAINST MULTIPLE ATTACKERS

"When facing multiple opponents you must attack first and keep attacking until the danger subdues."
Musasha.

Fighting/self-defence is not always about being fast, strong, accurate or even brave, though they are all, of course, important factors. It's about being 'first'. This is especially so in dealing with two, three or more attackers. If you're not first, you will most likely be last as we all know, 'last is lost' on the pavement arena. I have probably been involved in over 100 fights where I had to face more than one attacker, I won because I was first to initiate the 'physical' attack.

As detailed in Chapter 2 - 'Common Attack Scenarios', most assaults are preceded by verbal, it may be short to blunt, it may be long to elongated. Former or latter, it is present and you must act by attacking the attacker as quickly as you are sure an attack upon your person is imminent. With the lone attacker you may elongate the verbal whilst concentrating upon him and your pre-emptive 'line-up', with multiple attackers time is of the essence. The longer you take to analyse the situation and prepare, the less chance your pre-emptive attack has of being put into action, because the attackers will, gradually be surrounding you and getting closer in order to make their job a little easier, and yours increasingly harder. When they do attack, it will not be one at a time, each in succession, it will be all at once and brutally ferocious, leaving you very little chance of fighting back and very much chance of being hospitalised or killed.

Beware! For every 2-3 seconds (variable) that you delay your first pre-emptive strike you will be fighting one more opponent because by the second they will get closer. If you manage the pivotal seconds effectively your first attack will be to the opponent in front, then to the next close/

dangerous opponent. If you mismanage your allotted seconds your strategy must change. I call it the Red Letter syndrome. If you have 3 Red Letters (Bills) which do you pay first? You don't pay the one that fell through the letterbox this morning, you pay the one that has been in longest, the one that is threatening to 'cut you off'. So if you mismanage your time and the opponent on your left moves in closer then he becomes the opponent most dangerous (cut you off) and thus the first one you should attack, followed by the next closest. If the opponent on your right moves closer first then he is the one you must attack first. What usually occurs in these instances is the antagonists operate what the army would class as the 'pincer movement'. One, usually the one facing you, will deploy your attention whilst the other will attack you on your blind side. Deploy your vision and beware of this ploy.

The absolute pivotal factor in such a scenario is to attack first. Attack being your best means of defence. After your pre-emptive strike, it is best to make your getaway, if possible, if not, hit everything that moves and scream using 'Kiaa' to underline your resolve, to psyche out your antagonists and to attract attention to your dilemma. What weapon you use to attack is your own prerogative, whatever it is it should be your best shot aimed preferably at the vulnerables; eyes, throat, jaw, etc.

The photographs will illustrate the most common scenarios and how I have and would deal with them. Again it is impossible to cover every situation, because every situation is different in one way or another.

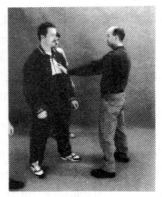

**Use lead hand to keep a safe distance, be submissive,
engage the opponent's brain and . . .**

. . . attack, right cross,

bridge the gap,

right cross again . . .

. . . and left hook.

Personally, my own pre-emptive strike would be a right cross/hook to the jaw preceded by some kind of mentally disarming verbal, hopefully rendering the first person unconscious, then I would attack with head, punch or kick to the remaining antagonists, depending upon my distance from them.

CHAPTER 18

THE KNOCK-OUT

"So in war, the way is to avoid what is strong and to strike at what is weak."
Sun Tzu.

The K.O. Impressive? Yes. Elusive? Not really. With the correct knowledge and the right technique it is very attainable. There are many contributing factors that combine and intermingle to form a knock-out on an adversary. Rising above all as the most important is not as you would imagine, a powerful strike, but an accurate one. A powerful attack that is not accurate is very unlikely to knock an adversary out. It is not, either, a matter of being big or heavy, size is irrelevant. An eight stone woman who punches her weight will have no trouble knocking an adversary unconscious if she is accurate.

The next important factor to accuracy is unexpectability. The adversary who does not expect the punch cannot prepare for the punch, therefore, the impetus of the punch is maximised. To attain a K.O. you rely heavily on the looseness of the adversary's neck and jaw muscles, if they are unbraced when you strike the jaw, a huge shaking of the adversary's brain will occur, it is this shaking of the brain that will bring on/cause unconsciousness. If, however, the adversary sees the strike coming, he will consciously/sub-consciously brace himself and the shaking is minimised and unconsciousness does not so readily occur. This is where we tie in with Chapter 7 - 'Line-ups'. The 'line-up' and verbal disarmament are pivotal in the execution of an effective K.O. The 'line-up' allows you to utilise your entire body weight from a stable, balanced posture, the verbal mental disarmament engages the adversary's brain for the split second it takes to launch your attack. While the brain is engaged, even for a second, the adversary will not see the punch/attack coming, because he doesn't see it coming, he does not brace himself for the strike, the jaw and neck muscles are relaxed, maximum shaking of the brain occurs followed closely by unconsciousness.

Anywhere along the line of the jaw bone, from the ear to the chin, if struck correctly, will cause the foregoing shaking of the brain that brings on unconsciousness. If you strike by the ear this will cause minimal shaking of the brain and a short spell of unconsciousness. The further down the jaw you strike the bigger the 'brain shake' and the larger the probability of unconsciousness, also, if unconsciousness does occur, the longer the spell of unconsciousness. By the same count, the further down the jaw you strike the smaller the target area becomes. A punch on the point of the jaw will have maximum effect.

The jaw bone when struck along the jaw line causes a shaking of the brain. However, when it is struck on the point of the chin the knockout occurs in two phases. First the clivius and the anterior edge of the occipital bone are pushed against the lower portions of the pons and the anterior surface of the medula oblongata. Next, by virtue of the 're-bounding effect', the medula oblongata bounces back against the internal surface of the occipital bone and the posterior edge of the foramen magnum. In essence, the double impact causes the medula oblongata, the most sensitive part of the brain, to concuss, thus causing temporary cancellation of the functions of the central nervous system.

The chances of such a strike are lessened by the fact that the target is only around one inch in diameter. I call it the 'Apple Tree' syndrome. If you shake an apple tree at the base of it's trunk, heavy shaking of the upper branches will occur, and lots of apples will fall. If, however, you shake the tree high up the trunk, minimal shaking of the upper branches will occur, and very few apples will fall. It is recommended, therefore, that you aim your blow at the middle of the jaw line (on the curve), where the target area is larger and the effect of an accurate blow will cause unconsciousness of a reasonable duration, certainly long enough to ensure getaway time.

The first thing to do, before you strike, is look at the target area on the jaw, if you do not, you are not likely to hit it. When you strike, do so with your best technique, preferably off the back leg to ensure body weight utilisation, (an experienced fighter may throw the technique off his front leg). Don't stop the punch and merely strike the target, punch through it with your blow and your body weight, (see illustrations).

A direct hit will cause unconsciousness in an adversary immediately, his fall will then add to his demur, because the unconscious head will usually meet the floor very heavily. If you are on target, but not right on the button, your adversary will, likely as not, fall to the floor in a semi-conscious stupor from which he usually recovers quite quickly, so get away as soon as possible. Even a blow that is off target should at least stun the adversary giving you enough time to run. Always, as a matter of course, try to verbally, mentally disarm and engage the adversary before you strike, this will greatly enhance the chances of a K.O. I would always, when possible, advise you to use a punching technique as opposed to anything else, because the hands are economical, fast and usually closer to the target (jaw), than most other attacking tools. When using the fist to strike, for best effect, strike the line of the jaw with the two major knuckles. If you cannot or do not use the fist then make sure you use the hardest part of whatever attacking tool you do use. 'Bone to bone' is always most effective. You may attack the jaw underneath (uppercut), around (hook), straight (cross), or overhand (hook), depending upon your preferences and strengths, all will have the desired effect if accurate, though, hooking punches seem to be the most effective.

So remember!

1. Line-up the adversary.
2. Mentally disarm him.
3. Look at the jaw.
4. Strike.
5. Follow through.

(As illustrated).

Disarm and engage the brain. Look at the jaw.

Strike and follow through with your bodyweight.

These are acquired techniques that, as always, must be practised. The focus pads, (as illustrated), are the most effective method of practising the K.O. You may also practice with control, on a partner. Practice as though it were real, including the verbal, mental disarmament for best effect.

CHAPTER 19

HURDLES AND PITFALLS

"Nothing of any value ever came without a fight."

This chapter is aimed, in the main, at the practising martial artists, but the values and theories herein cover a far wider spectrum, because no matter what it is you are trying to achieve in life, whether it is competence to excellence in the martial arts, faster track times in the world of athletics, building up a successful business or even maintaining a healthy relationship with your spouse, you are always going to have the hindrance of hurdles and pitfalls.

The old addage of 'no pain, no gain' is without doubt the truth. The mind is like an overbearing parent, frightened to give his child too much control, as soon as you are starting to gain a little competence and get a little way up the mountain of self-realisation, it (the mind), throws something tangible or intangible in your way to slow you down or stop you completely, because the further you get up that mountain and the more hurdles you climb over and pitfalls you cross the stronger you get and the more control over your own mind you attain.

At the top of the mountain is the ultimate goal of complete mind control. On the way up you will have developed, because of your overthrow of the hurdles and pitfalls, an iron will and an indomitable spirit. Also gained would be enlightenment, because in order to get over some of the more difficult hurdles and pitfalls, it is necessary to mentally dissect yourself admitting and recognising your weaknesses in order to be able to confront and overcome them, and thus, get past whatever stumbling block it is that's holding you back. This mental dissection is what brings you enlightenment. This is why hurdles and pitfalls are, in essence, a God send, because without the challenge of them, you wouldn't find enlightenment, you would not develop the iron will that is necessary to confront them nor the indomitable spirit that is develop by never giving in to them when the going gets tough.

The 'journey' is, metaphorically speaking, like a bowl of water, you are like an inflated bicycle innertube. You immerse the innertube (yourself), into the water (the journey), to find out, via the bubbles, where there are any leaks (your own weaknesses). Once you have found the leaks and you know where they are, you can patch them up until, ultimately, you have no leaks.

The aforementioned hurdles and pitfalls are or can be many splendoured. They may be tangible or intangible. Sometimes when there are no hurdles imminent, the mind, wishing to abort the journey, will invent silly ones. Basically speaking, hurdles and pitfalls come in three categories, though are uniform in one element, they are all reasons to give in, and are nearly always thrown in when the recipient is just starting to gain some kind of realisation and competence. Recognising them as hurdles and pitfalls and realising that the real benefits to be had from training are gained only by overcoming them, will help immeasurably in your bid to do so.

The three categories of reasons not to continue the metaphoric journey are Tangible, Intangible and Silly reasons.

Tangible Reasons:
These are incidental hurdles and pitfalls that are responsible for more 'lay offs' from training than any other reason. Broken bones, torn ligaments, twisted ankles, illnesses (one of my students once missed two months training because, and I quote, "Me mum's got to 'ave an 'isterectomy''), the list goes on. With a serious injury it is foolish to keep training as the injury/illness may be aggravated by your continuance. However, minor injuries should not deter you from conscientious practice. You can quite easily train around such injuries. If your left hand is injured, train your right or vice versa. I was in and out of hospital, and plaster, for two years and had, in that time, two operations for a broken right wrist. I never missed training once and used the time to perfect my left hand techniques. I have also had broken bones all over my body, but

still managed to train around my injuries. Training under such adverse conditions requires and develops real will-power and is a great character builder.

With the more serious injury/illness that does lay you off, the danger lies in whether or not you get back to training after your convalescence. From my experience, most people do not. While you are recovering try to visit your training establishment to maintain your ties and enthusiasm, this will greatly help in your re-start program when the obstacle of bad health is removed. A lot of people use their injuries to opt out because they were finding the going getting tough anyway, but remember this, if it was easy everybody and his dog would be walking around with a black belt tied to his waist. If there is no adversity there is no advance.

Intangible Reasons:
These can be as destructive in your advancement as the tangibles and in a psychological sense far more painful. Also, because they are mental as opposed to physical, they can quite often by very difficult to admit or detect. The greatest intangible is 'physical contact', sparring or getting hit. A great percentage of people leave training because they are frightened of sparring. Even at the boxing club when I was coaching, it was common knowledge that you lost 85% of your new starters after you put them in the ring for the first time. The only way to overcome this fear is to confront it again and again until you become desensitised to it, and take heart, it does get better. The more you sparr and put yourself in the firing line the better and more confident you will feel. In the world of real fighting ,pain, unfortunately, is the ugly hand maiden, so it is imperative that you develop at least some tolerance for it if you want any chance of surviving a real situation.

Boredom:
"It's getting boring." If I had a penny for every time I've heard this excuse! Boredom is another major pitfall that loses many people from the martial arts arena and in my opinion, it is a lazy excuse. To develop a technique into an instinctive reflex, to develop power, speed, endurance, footwork or anything else worth having for that matter, requires repetition, and what is repetition if it isn't boring. Repetition is practised

by the student revising for his doctorate, and paradoxically, by the soldier perfecting a bayonet attack. Swimmers will practice hours and hours a day perfecting a stroke and jugglers will juggle until their hands bleed, all in pursuit of excellence. As martial artists, we are no different. For one technique to be effective in a 'live' situation we must do a thousand in the gym. Boredom is the lazy mans excuse not to train. You must treat boredom as another challenge, hurdle or pitfall that must be bettered if advancement is to be attained. When boredom sets in you must use concentration to push it back out again. Sheer concentration on the technique you are practising will erode boredom. You must practice a technique until you are sick to death of it, then you will get good at it.

Lack of Enjoyment:
Lack of enjoyment in training is brothers with boredom. Another feeble excuse. Enjoyment in training comes and goes, nobody enjoys it all of the time. The real enjoyment comes from the fruits of training rather than the actual training itself. After all, to become proficient we must push ourselves through the pain of a gruelling training session, who in their right mind enjoys pain, (my profuse apologies to all you masochists out there!). If you are going through a bad patch of not enjoying your training, stick with it and try to treat the training as a mundane task that has to be done, the enjoyment will return. It's unrealistic to expect enjoyment all the time out of something so physically and mentally demanding, when the enjoyment is there make the best of it, when it isn't cope. It's all part of the character building process.

Lack of Improvement:
Another favourite excuse for throwing in the towel is, "I don't seem to be getting any better." This is one of the mind's most excellent finishers and kills off many students with the suddenness of cyanide tea, after all, what is the point of continuing in training if you're not getting any better? If I may use a metaphor, it is like a propelling spiral that picks up momentum very quickly, just as it seems to be reaching it's pinnacle of speed, it starts, or at least it would appear, going backwards. So it is with the martial arts, in the beginning you are learning something new every session and improvement can be as fast as the aforementioned

metaphoric spiral. All of a sudden your advancement seems to be slowing down and in some cases you seem, (like the spiral), to be going backward instead of forward, but it is only an illusion. After such a quick advance even a slight decrease in speed may seem like a backward spiral, usually it is only the person himself who sees or thinks he sees this supposed decline, everyone else around him will be seeing his improvement but him. From my experience and as irony would have it, it is usually the better student who thinks he isn't improving. Every day and every session that you train will bring you, visible or invisible, large or small, some advancement. The child that you see everyday will show no visible change or growth, to the person who only sees the same child every few months, the change is so obvious that they sometimes can't believe it's the same child. And so it is with improvement in training, sometimes it is so gradual that on a day to day basis it is almost unnoticeable, but it will be there.

Silly Reasons:
These are the most infuriating and are always employed by people who are using the 'silly excuse' to cover a deeper, more underlying reason or problem, probably one of those in the last category. These are the worst, (and sometimes the funniest) reasons for missing single sessions or even packing in all together, because it means that the person employing the 'silly excuse' cannot come to terms with the real reason.

To my mind this put him right at the bottom of the proverbial mountain with a long, long way to go, he'll probably never make it. Here are my favourite 'silly' reasons all of which have been used to me over the years.

"I can't train because . . ."

1. My cat died. (A great excuse because it can be used nine times).

2. My mother is having a hysterectomy. (I think he was getting sympathy pains.)

3. My suit is in the wash. (As coincidence would have it, the Cup final coincided with my training time, this way just one of the many excuses used that night.)

4. I haven't got any money. (Saw him in the pub drunk later that night.)

5. My grandad died. (Third time this year.)

6. I had to go to a funeral. (Hope it's not his grandad again.)

7. My wife's ill. (It would be a good excuse if he didn't use it every fortnight.)

8. It was raining. (He must be made of sugar.)

9. My mums varicose veins are playing her up. (What?)

10. I can't take my grading because my flat's flooded and my daughter fell off her bike. (The grading wasn't for another 6 weeks.)

Every reason not to train, with a few exceptions, can be turned into a reason to train. The real strength to be attained is hidden within the hurdles and pitfalls, if you want that strength then you have to overcome and defeat them.

CHAPTER 20

VISUALISATION

"Seeing is achieving! Whatever the mind of man can conceive he can achieve."

"It's been said that imagination is stronger than will-power and by not trying, by just visualising the goal accomplished it can be easier to achieve in real life."
Takayuki Kubota.

Top golfers are unanimous in their praise for it, champion body builders put it 'en par' with diet, and it is used with great success universally by doctors and psychologists, yet is still lies, largely in the shadow of disbelief and ignorance. Some skeptics may laugh at the very thought of programming your mind, via visualisation, but who can argue with documented fact (or Tak Kubota for that matter). I think that visualisation is best summed up by the 'Samuels & Samuels (Who?) statement, "What people visualise is what they get, likewise, what they have is a result of what they have visualised".

Visualisation.

Visualisation is a many splendoured thing in that it can be used to attain many things, from building up confidence to perfecting technique to confronting fears. In a documented experiment in America, (one of many putting visualisation to the test), two groups of students were given the task of practising basket-ball penalty shots everyday for a month. One group actually physically practised netting the ball whilst the other group lay on a bed or sat in a chair and, using visualisation, mentally practised netting the ball. At the end of the month both groups met up at a basket-ball court and physically competed to see which of the two could net the most shots. The group that had practised using visualisation won by a considerable margin. That isn't to say that you should replace physical practice with visualisation, but certainly use it as a strong supplement. In a combat sense I have successfully commissioned the use of visualisation on many occasions, and genuinely believe that almost anything is attainable through its conscientious practice.

"All we have is a result of what we have thought", Dhamnapada (psychologist). Many top martial arts competitors are starting to latch onto visualisation and the benefits it can offer. Chuck Norris, in his competition days, used it before he fought and said that many times he scored points on his opponent's with the exact moves he had beaten them with, in his minds eye, only minutes before.

Floro Villabrille, the famous, unbeaten Filipino martial artist who was the victor of countless full contact Escrima and Kali matches practised visualisation whilst he actually trained. He would always go up to the mountains, alone, before a match and in his imagination would fight his opponent over and over again until he felt he couldn't lose. He was quoted as saying, "I can't lose, when I enter the ring nobody can beat me, I already know that man is beaten."

Before I actually go into the practice methods of visualisation let us first examine what the famous humanistic psychologist, Abraham Moslow, termed the 'Jonah Complex', or in layman's terms, the fear of success.

You may be surprised to learn that the 'Jonah Complex' stifles the advancement of as many people as the fear of failure. Moslow also stated, "We are generally afraid to become that which we can glimpse in our most perfect moments, under the most perfect conditions, under conditions of greatest courage, we enjoy and even thrill to the God-like possibilities we see in ourselves at such peak moments, and yet, simultaneously, shiver with weakness, awe and fear before the same possibilities". How very true! Many people would, for instance, enjoy the prestige of representing the K.U.G.B. national squad, but how many of those same people, I wonder, would relish the thought of facing the like of Ronnie (the Tasmanian devil) Christopher and others of his ilk at squad meetings once a month. Not so many I think! So, be careful of that for which you dream, for your dreams may come true.

METHODS OF PRACTICE

Visual rehearsal, self actualisation, going to the movies or visualisation, call it what you will, the process is basically the same and really quite a simple way of utilising a little more of your 'mental muscle'.

Initially, the best way of practising visualisation is lying down in a quiet, darkened room. Close your eyes, breath in and out deeply and relax. Once a relaxed state is acquired try to picture in your minds eye the goal desired. At first you might find this difficult, but, with practice it will get easier and the mental images clearer.

Picture yourself facing your fear or performing that trophy winning Kata again and again, until it is well and truly programmed into that computer we call 'our brain'. Try to see the desired goal in as much detail as possible. The brain finds it very difficult to discern between what is imagined and what is actual, all it knows is what is programmed into it, so when you come to perform the goal that you've visualised, the brain gets straight into gear because you've rehearsed it so much it thinks it has done it before, and face the bully, performs the perfect Kata, or whatever, without demur.

Most people only partially practice visualisation in that they only use one of the senses (imagined senses), i.e. sight, out of the possible five. Psychologists talk of the three out of five rule. Using three out of your five senses, they say, will enhance your visualisation practice. Tom Platze, 'Mr Legs', one of the world's greatest body builders says, and I quote, ''If you can use five of your senses in visualisation practice I'm confident that you can triple the results of your visualisation process''. For instance, if you employ the three out of five rule, and as a hypothetical example your desired goal is to successfully defend yourself in a self-defence scenario, imagine the 'feel' of fear within you and confidently, controlling that fear. The 'sight' and 'sound' of your potential attacker before you, the 'sound' of your reticent voice refusing to balk to his threats, and perhaps as a climax see, hear and feel yourself neutralising him with your well practised pre-emptive strike, the sound of his body falling, the 'sound' of your feet running away.

The more real and the more detailed you make your imagined per-formance the better your results will be. I often practice just before I go out to work as a doorman in the night clubs. Mentally rehearsing techniques that have been successful for me in the past, (it's always easier to visualise something that you have done/experienced before). In this sense I have found its practice an invaluable asset.

As a final note, if you have trouble visualising images try 'going to the movies'. In your minds eye imagine a huge cinema screen in front of you, on the screen picture yourself scoring ippon with jodan mawashigeri or confronting the bully, etc, make the image as vivid as possible, use the three out of five rule and repeat the sequence as often as you can (15 minutes per day) and it will, eventually become programmed into your mind. But please remember it is not a substitute, rather an additive to physical training.

CHAPTER 21

AFTERMATH

"He who wishes to fight must first count the cost."
Sun Tzu.

As if the trauma of an attack isn't enough, afterwards follows the aftermath of emotion which can often leave a scar on the psyche that will long outlast any physical scars incurred. Some victims of robbery, burglary and rape, etc, never emotionally recover. Victims of burglaries are often so incensed by the crime that they cannot bear to live in the house any longer, so sell up and move, then often still live in constant fear of a burglary to their new home, especially older people who have not the will or constitution to fight this corroding emotion. Rape victims, especially the ones who were too frightened to fight back, are often the worst hit by this intangible phenomenon that has driven many to nervous breakdowns, insanity and even suicide. Victims of unsolicited violence are often, as an after effect, too frightened to go out alone and live under the dominion of that fear for many years, some for life.

The stress of the aftermath often takes its toll on the family unit, sometimes, especially in rape cases, causing divorce or separation, then later problems with new spouses and new families. Victims of rape often live with a terrible underlying feeling of guilt, believing that perhaps in some perverse way it was all their own fault. Of course, the blame for this sickening crime (rape), is never and can never by apportioned to the victim. Much of the guilt stems from the fact that the victim feels as though she did not fight off the attacker with enough zest, the feeling is then re-emphasised when in court, (if it ever gets to court, a third of rape cases are not even reported), the rapist's defending council verbally rips the victim to pieces and attacks her with insulting and insinuating questions, suggesting that she condoned and enjoyed the act and that, in fact, his client (the rapist), is really the victim. The court case for the victim, can often be more demanding and damaging than the rape itself.

All victims of physical attack, across the board, can expect mild to severe depression after the fact. A severe loss of confidence may be experienced along with temper tantrums and severe mood swings. Sometimes spates of elongated crying spells may occur for no apparent reason. Often the feeling of unworthiness and a depressing lack of hope, as though the future is full of doom and gloom. I have been in many bad situations and have experienced many of these feelings, sometimes they all fuse together and you don't know what it is you're feeling, only that it's bad. Even when you successfully defend yourself you may still get bouts of depression and gloom. I'm not a medical person, so I would not presume to tell you how to overcome these feelings. With me it is, or has been, a way of life and these feelings, as unwelcome as they are, are very common to me, this familiarity loses the feelings' impetus so I can handle them better than most. If you feel like crying, then cry, even deliberately watch a sad film to bring the tears on, because crying is very therapeutic. The tears contain a hormone release that will help you to feel better, it is nature's way of releasing the bad emotions from your body that may otherwise lie trapped. In the long term, trapped emotions can have a very detrimental effect developing into psychosomatic illnesses, ulcers, angina and bad nerves. So do not harbour the tears, let them flow. The aftermath may be little more than mild depression which you may feel capable of handling, if the symptoms are more severe you should consult you own G.P. or talk to your loved ones, 'A problem shared is a problem halved'.

The main aim of this chapter is to enlighten you, again, 'Forewarned is forearmed'. If you expect the aftermath and prepare yourself mentally, its impetus is greatly lost.

CHAPTER 22

CASE HISTORIES

In my research for this book I talked to and interviewed many people. I spoke to victims of attack and also to muggers. The following two interviews are typical of all the interviews that I conducted, printed here with kind permission of the interviewees.

I found the interviews enlightening and deeply thought provoking, I could, quite easily have filled a whole book with such interviews, but that would be out of context of this book. I leave you to draw your own conclusions from the interviews, I hope you can, as I have, learn from them.

THE VICTIMS

"If you have been shown, offered, yet still refused the armour of awareness do not gripe when you are slain due to its lack."

The first interview was conducted 1 month after the incident, with James McKay from Nuneaton, West Midlands, who was one of three young men attacked in August 1992, by a group of seven men in their late twenties.

James is 6ft 1" tall, weighs 11 st and attends technical college, he is also a part-time window cleaner.

Matthew is 20 years old, 5ft 11" tall and stockily built.

Dominic is 19 years old, 5ft 11" tall and of average build.

James is the interviewee:

Q. James, would you mind telling me about the night you and your friends were attacked?

A. No, not at all. Me and my friends went out to the local pub on the Saturday night for a bit of a drink at about 9.00 pm. We met some girls at the pub and were getting on really well with them. We were having a good night. We left the girls, and the pub, at about 10.45 pm to go for the last drink at another pub, further up the road. On the way to the pub we had to walk down a country lane and over a small bridge with steep grass banks either side of us. Seven men, well about seven, aged between 22-30 ran up either side of the bank toward us.

Q. How long did it take them to get up the banks and reach you?

A. About 5-10 seconds. It was pitch black and we didn't know what was going on.

Q. At this stage did you feel scared?

A. No, not really, we just thought that they were running up to the path. Then one of them punched me in the ribs, that's when I got scared. Looking back, it was obvious what they were going to do, we just didn't think.

Q. Did you 'freeze'?

A. Yes, I think so. I got punched in the eye, it wasn't a hard punch, it just shocked me.

Q. What happened then?

A. I was punched a few times, then thrown down one of the banks. I got up and ran home.

Q. Why did you run home?

A. I just felt really scared, I didn't want to be there.

Q. What happened to your mates?

A. When I got home I rang Dominic and Matthew to see how they were. They both had black eyes and bruised faces. They were more worried about me than themselves, because I was the youngest.

Q. How did the feel mentally?

A. They felt alright, just pissed off that they were attacked for nothing.

Q. How did you feel?

A. Basically O.K. I felt a bit of a coward for running. I felt like I'd let my mates, and myself down, and I felt like I'd let my parents down too.

Q. Why?

A. Because my dad has always taught me that I should always stick-up for myself.

Q. And you feel as though you didn't do enough?

A. Yes.

Q. In retrospect, what could you have done to avoid the attack?

A. We could have taken a different route to the pub, where we were attacked was really secluded. If we'd have gone a different way it would never have happened.

Q. What about the fight itself. What would you have done differently?

A. Well, looking back, when the blokes ran up the banks we had plenty of chance to run, or even if we didn't run I could have punched one of them in the face. I used to box so I can hit quite hard. I should have hit him before he hit me.

Q. What about the fear? How would you overcome the feeling that made you 'freeze'.

A. Last time I wasn't calm, next time I'd try to stay calm and try to hit one of them before I got hit.

Q. How did your parents and friends react to you being attacked?

A. My parents were really worried, but I told them I was alright. My dad said I was lucky, I could have been badly hurt or killed.

Q. Did your dad say that you should have fought back?

A. No, no, he understood. He was just glad that I was alright.

Q. What about your friends?

A. Some of them called me a puff and a coward because I didn't fight back, but they weren't there, it's not as easy as you think?

Q. What are your thoughts on those who called you names?

A. I don't think they'd do any better, in fact when I asked some of them to come and help me get the blokes the next week, they all made excuses why they couldn't make it.

Q. They bottled out?

A. Yes.

Q. Now it's all behind you, how do you feel?

A. It still bugs me that I didn't fight back. I wouldn't have minded getting beaten up so much if I'd have had a 'go' back.

Q. So that still plays on your mind?

A. Yes. It bugs me.

Q. Do you know why you were attacked?

A. No. The only thing I can think is that they might have seen us talking to the girls in the pub and not like it.

Q. What steps have you taken to ensure that you are better prepared next time?

A. I'm going back to boxing and I've started weight lifting.

Q. What about the mental side?

A. Boxing and weight training are building up my confidence a lot. I feel much stronger mentally.

Q. Is there any advice you would like to offer people reading this interview?

A. Only that I hope they learn from my mistakes and take precautions now, before it happens, and not to be ashamed to run away if they have the chance.

THE ATTACKERS

"Knowing the enemy enables you to take the offensive." Sun Tzu.

The two attackers that I interviewed wished to remain anonymous. They both earned their living from crime, more specifically robbery with violence (mugging), accosting up to 8 victims in any one night.

J and P both began their criminal careers at the age of 13, they are now 17, and at the time of this interview serving 4 years for robbery with violence. Both are 6ft 2" tall with slim to medium build.

Q. J., P., why do you commit these offences?

A. J. For money, and the buzz.
P. It's a good laugh.

Q. What time do you instigate your attacks?

A. J and P. At night.

Q. Why not in the day?

A. J. Too many people about. Too easy to get caught.

Q. How do you choose your victims?

A. J and P. Student types, men carrying umbrellas or wearing glasses, usually aged between 20-30, occasionally older. We also look for people who are well dressed, smart clothes means money.

Q. Why those particular types of people?

A. P. Because they always have money or cards, and they don't give you any hassle.

Q. What happens after you have chosen a victim?

A. P. We follow them, cross the road, walk passed them may be two or three times. Some of them must be thick not to notice what's going on.

Q. What is your next move?

A. J and P. We wait for them to walk into a side street or walk into a park, anywhere quiet. We walk up to them and ask the time, this distracts them while we pull out our knifes. When they look up we say, ''Give us your fucking money!'' They usually look blank. Both of us shout at them, ''Get your fucking wallet out'', and put the knives closer to their face.

Q. Then what?

A. P. They get their money out and offer you some, but I snatch the lot.

Q. What if they have no money?

A. J and P. We take their jewellery.

Q. What if they have no jewellery, either?

A. J and P. We laugh and say, "See you later", then run off.

Q. What do you do with the money, credit cards and jewellery.

A. P. I spend the cash on drink, sell the cards for £50 each and the jewellery, unless it's something I like, then I keep it.

Q. So you have a drink in between muggings?

A. P. Yeah!

Q. Is there anybody that you would not mug?

A. P and J. Old women, kids.

Q. What do mean, kids?

A. Under 12's.

Q. Anybody else?

A. P and J. We don't like doing drunks.

Q. Why, I thought drunks would be easy targets?

A. P and J. They are, but a lot of them don't take you seriously, they could fall on the knife or something and that could mean a 25 stretch (25 years in prison).

Q. What would cause you to stop an attack once you've started.

A. P. If they scream or if they fuck about.

Q. What do you mean, 'fuck about'?

A. J. Start giving you hassle, like pretending to look for their money, taking their time, arguing. There was this old geezer who we were just about to 'do', when he turned into his drive. We stopped him and told him to give us his money, but he just kept on walking to his door. We thought he was deaf, but when he got to his door he turned round and told us to 'fuck off'. That really blew me man.

Q. Does the size of the victim matter.

A. P and J. No.

Q. What would put you off?

A. P. Build, someone who's stocky or if they look mean, the sound of their voice.

Q. What do you mean?

A. P and J. When you ask them the time, if they sound tough.

Q. Explain that more.

A. P. Well, if, when you get close to them they look a bit tough, when you ask them the time if they answer with a rough voice, then we just walk off.

Q. How do you feel when you are looking for a victim?

A. P and J. Nervous, high, on a buzz.

Q. How do you feel when your mugging someone?

A. P. Calm.
J. I'm just laughing to myself.
P. I'm in control, I'm looking around thinking of getting away.

Q. How do you feel after?

A. P. A great buzz, the more daring it is the more buzz I get. I get round the corner and collapse with laughter. My hands are shaking and my knees are weak, I have to sit down. Then we go and buy some drink.

Q. How many people do you mug in one night?

A. P and J. We have done 8, but most times about 6. If we get a lot of money the first or second time we get too drunk to do anymore.

Q. How much cash do you get in one night?

A. P. The most is about £80, but usually £40.

Q. Can you give me a typical example of one of your attacks?

A. P. There was this geezer and his Mrs, outside a telephone box. Their car had the bonnet up, the woman went into the phone box. We walked up to the phone box and pretended to queue for the phone. The geezer looked like he had money, good clothes, smart car. I gave J. the signal by winking at him, I then asked the geezer the time and we both pulled out our knives. When he looked up we told him to hand over his wallet. He said, "Do you know who I am?" I said, "I don't care who you are. He said, "Do you know who she's on the phone to (indicating to his wife in the phone box), the Police." This was taking too long I thought to myself, I said, "I'm going to give you to the count of three, or else", and pushed the knife closer to his throat. He handed over his wallet and we ran off. All the time this was happening the woman on the phone didn't realise what was going on.

Q. What would you have done if he hadn't have handed over his wallet?

A. J and P. Run.

Q. Have you any mates that do the same sort of thing as you?

A. P. Most of our mates are into mugging and crime.

Q. Do they all operate the same system?

A. J and P. Sort of.

Q. What do you mean?

A. J and P. Well, we all learn off each other, some use bats, iron bars or pretend guns, other use knives like us.

Q. Do all of your mates run off if they come up against problems or complications?

A. P. Yeah. You can't afford to be caught mugging, look what happened to us, 4 years each.

CHAPTER 23

DO'S AND DON'TS

"He will win who knows how to handle both superior and inferior forces."

In the foregoing chapters we have covered a lot of the things that you should and should not adhere to. Here I'd like to list a few of the more important points to bear in mind. Again they are only suggestions and your prerogative is your own, but please don't say I didn't warn you.

1 Don't get too drunk.
Alcohol in moderation is fine. If you drink too much, however, you are an easy target for attackers. Alcohol temporarily erodes the balance, distancing, sight, sound, in fact nearly every sense is impaired. You also fail to see danger when drunk and cannot, even if very proficient, expect to realistically defend yourself whilst under the influence.

2 Don't underestimate an adversary.
Confidence is a great attribute, over-confidence is a very weak link. Never allow yourself to underestimate anyone, it is a sure sign, on your part, of over-confidence and over-confidence begets defeat. If you start feeling too confident about a situation remind yourself of the possible dangers you are facing. Better to be a little under-confident than over-confident.

3 Be basic.
Never employ a technique for the sake of dramatic effect. Looking good counts for nothing, many people have lost trying to look good. Use the quickest, most basic and economical technique available to you.

4 Be quick.
Don't hang around. If you're going to attack a potential attacker do so as soon as possible, especially when dealing with more than one

adversary. Any time delay in pre-emptively attacking will lessen your chances of success.

5 Be hard.

Do not allow sentiment to enter into your mind when dealing with a potential attacker, he will manipulate and engineer any chink in your mental armour, until it is a cavernous opening that he can walk straight through. When dealing with 'bad' people you have to be as 'bad' as them if you want to survive. At least for the duration of the attack.

6 Don't be suckered.

Be very sceptical of an adversary offering to shake hands or plea bargain, it is very often a ploy to 'sucker' you into an attack. If you do accept, do so warily. The same ploy is often worked by an adversary offering a cigarette and then striking out as the person receives it.

7 Kill your pride.

Pride has no place in self-defence. If you can run away from a situation or talk your way out of a fight, do it. Survival is all that matters.

8 Don't be squeamish.

If sticking your fingers in an adversary's eyes is what you have to do to survive an attack, do it, don't be squeamish or you'll lose.

9 Kill fair play.

When an attack on your person is in progress or imminent, there is no such thing as fair play. Do anything and use anything to defend yourself. There is only one rule, there are none.

10 Never do more than is necessary.

In defending yourself, it is imperative that you 'hit and run'.
Don't hang around trying to 'finish the job'. As soon as you can, run. It is not unheard of for a stunned adversary, even a felled one, to recover and still beat the victim who is close enough to grab.

CHAPTER 24

FIRST AID

In the execution of self-defence it is quite likely that you, even if you defend yourself successfully, may pick up minor or serious injuries. You may be with a friend or friends who are injured or you may even wish to treat an attacker who you have injured in the process of defending yourself. Although the latter is unlikely and not recommended, not to be unchristian about it, more to be realistic, once your adversary has been stopped it is highly dangerous to hang around. Though, of course, the prerogative is entirely yours.

The Principle of First Aid.

First aid is the skilled application of accepted methods of treatment on the occurrence of an injury or in the case of sudden illness, using facilities or materials available at the time. It is the approved method of treating a casualty until placed, if necessary, in the care of a doctor or removed to hospital.

First aid treatment is given to sustain life.

To prevent his condition from becoming worse.

To promote recovery.

So basically, if the injuries are bad, you are looking to do a patch-up job that will suffice until somebody skilled, i.e. a doctor or hospital can take over. Of course, injuries sustained in physical attacks can be very multi-various, so we will try to aim at the obvious and potentially life threatening injuries.

The Scope of First Aid.

This consists of four parts:
1. Assessing the situation.
2. Diagnosing what is wrong.
3. Giving immediate and appropriate treatment.
4. Disposing the casualty to a doctor, hospital or home, according to the seriousness of the situation.

In the attack scenario, from my experience the most common injuries are unconsciousness, face and head wounds and stab wounds to the body.

Unconscious Casualty.
If the casualty is unconscious the task of ascertaining his/her injuries is a difficult one because you cannot ask the person where he hurts, etc, (well you can, but he is unlikely to answer!). So, a thorough detailed examination of the person is necessary. Note if breathing is present. If absent, immediately commence artificial respiration, (as shown in illustration).

Examine over and under the casualty for dampness which might indicate bleeding or incontinence. Stop any serious bleeding before proceeding further with the examination. Bear in mind the possibilities of internal bleeding. Once everything is in order, breathing, etc, place the casualty in the recovery position, (as illustrated).

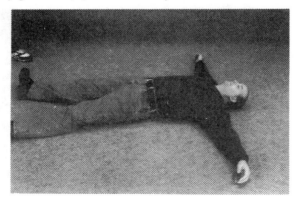

Unconsciousness.

The Recovery Position.

If the casualty is lying on his/her back:

1 Kneel beside him/her and place both his/her arms close to his/her body. Cross his/her far leg over his/her near leg. Protect his/her face with one of your hands. Gently turn the casualty onto his/her side. This may be done by grasping the casualty's attire at the hip.

2 Draw up the upper arm until it makes a right angle to the body and bend at the elbow.

3 Draw up the upper leg until the thigh makes a right angle to the body and bend the knee.

4 Draw out the underneath arm gently backward to extend it slightly behind his back.

5 Bend the undermost knee slightly.

The reason for the limbs being placed in this manner is that it provides the necessary stability to keep the casualty comfortable in the recovery position, and stop him/her from rolling onto his/her back, where he/she may choke. If the casualty is very heavy, two hands may be used to grip the clothing and in this instance you should kneel at the side of the casualty so that when he/she is turned, his/her face will rest against your knees. If bystanders are present, employ their assistance with the turning. Gently tilt the casualty's head slightly back so as to ensure an open airway.

The recovery position.

Artificial Respiration.

There are many methods of artificial respiration. The most effective is mouth to mouth, (mouth to nose), and this method can be used by almost all age groups and in almost all circumstances except when there is severe injury to the face and mouth, when the casualty is vomiting and it interferes with respiratory resuscitation.

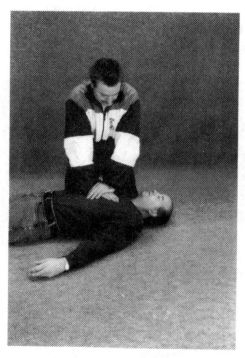

Artificial respiration.

Treatment.

1 Ensure the casualty has a good airway by tilting back the head. Support the back of the neck and press the top of the head so that it is tilted backward, simultaneously press the chin upward. This will extend the head/neck and lift the tongue forward clear of the airway. This is particularly vital if the casualty is on his/her back, because the tongue may fall to the back of the throat and cause him/her to swallow his/her tongue.

2 Loosen the casualty's clothing at the neck and waist. If the casualty is not breathing keep the head tilted backward and begin mouth to mouth, (mouth to nose), breathing.

3 Open you mouth wide and take a deep breath. Pinch the casualty's nose together using your thumb and forefinger. Seal your lips around the casualty's mouth. Blow into the lungs until the chest rises then remove your mouth and watch the chest fall. Continue these inflations at the natural rate of breathing. Continue until the casualty begins breathing on his/her own.

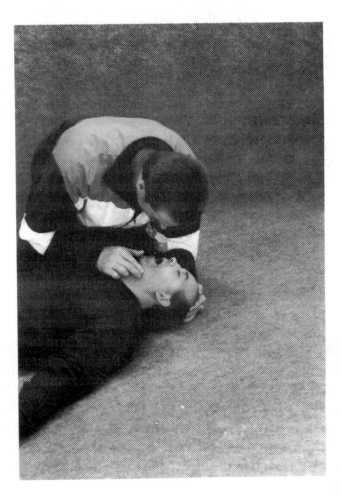

Mouth to mouth.

If you can't make a seal around the casualty's mouth, you may try mouth to nose. You may wish to place a handkerchief over the casualty's mouth for hygiene reasons. If the casualty's heart is not beating and his/her colour becomes blue/grey, his/her pupils are widely dilated and you cannot feel a pulse, put him/her on his/her back on a flat surface and strike the chest sharply to the lower part of the breast bone with the edge of the hand, hopefully this will restart the heart. If not, start external heart compressions whilst at the same time continuing to give artificial respiration, (see illustrations).

1 Take up position at the side of the casualty.

2 Find the lower half of the breast bone.

3 Place the heel of your hand on this part of the bone, keeping the palm and the fingers off the chest.

4 Cover this hand with the heel of the other.

5 With the arms straight, rock forward pressing down on the lower half of the breast bone, (about 1 to 1) inches in). Adult casualty - repeat the pressure once per second. Make sure the pressure you push with is controlled, too much pressure may cause damage to the casualty's ribs or internal organs.

6 Check your effectiveness by watching for an improvement in the casualty's colour, noticing the size of his/her pupils which should become smaller with effective treatment and feeling for a progressively stronger pulse.

7 In extreme cases, this method should be continued until help arrives. The rate of lung inflation, (mouth to mouth), and heart compressions should be 15 heart compressions followed by two quick lung inflations, and then repeat until the casualty's heart and breath return or help arrives.

Stab Wounds.

Potentially, a fatal place to be stabbed, a wound in the chest may well allow direct access of air into the chest cavity. When you (or whoever it is who has been stabbed), breathes in, the noise of air may be heard. When you breath out, blood or blood-stained bubbles may be expelled from the wound. If the lung is injured, you (the casualty), may also cough up frothy bright red blood. The immediate aim is to seal up the wound and stop air entering the chest cavity. Until a dressing can be applied, place the palm of the hand firmly over the wound, lay down (the casualty), with head and shoulders raised and the body inclined toward the injured side. If there is first aid equipment available, plug the wound lightly with a dressing, then cover the dressing with a thick layer of cotton wool. Keep it in place by strapping or a bandage. Get hospital help urgently.

Wounds to the stomach. (Abdominal wall)

Place the casualty so that the wound does not gape, preferably on his back with head and shoulders raised and supported with a pillow under his knees. If there are no internal organs protruding apply a dressing to the wound, (if one is available), and bandage it firmly into position. If internal organs are protruding, cover them lightly with a soft, clean towel or a large gauze dressing, secure without undue pressure. If the casualty is coughing or vomiting, be sure to support the abdomen. Generally speaking, with profuse bleeding to miscellaneous body parts, apply firm pressure with a towel or gauze and try to elevate the body part that is bleeding, i.e. leg, arm, etc, and keep the pressure fixed until the bleeding stops or professional help arrives. If the bleeding cannot be controlled by the application of pressure on the wound, or when it is impossible to apply direct pressure, it is sometimes possible to apply indirect pressure at the appropriate pressure point between the heart and the wound.

A pressure point is where an important artery can be compressed against an underlying bone to prevent the flow of blood beyond that point. Such pressure may be applied while dressing, pad and bandage are being prepared for application, but not for longer than 15 minutes at a time.

Brachial pressure point.

The Brachial artery runs along the inner side of the muscle of the upper arm, it's course being roughly indicated by the inner seam of a coat sleeve. To apply pressure, pass your fingers under the casualty's upper arm and compress the artery against the bone.

Femoral pressure point.

The Femoral artery passes into the lower limb at a point corresponding to the fold of the groin. To apply pressure behind the casualty's knee, grasp his thigh with both hands and press directly and firmly downward in the centre of the groin with both thumbs, one on top of the other against the brim of the pelvis.

Bleeding from the nose.

Sit the casualty down with his head slightly forward and tell him to breath through his mouth. Pinch the soft part of the nose firmly for about 8-10 minutes. Loosen his clothing about the neck and chest and warn him against trying to blow his nose.

All the former treatments may easily be applied to yourself as well as any other casualty occurring from the attack by following the instructions laid out. In serious cases, or if in doubt always get hospital treatment.

CHAPTER 25

SELF DEFENCE AND THE LAW

"He will win who has military capacity and is not interfered with by the sovereign."
Sun Tzu.

Before I delve into the histrionics of the law and how you the victim stands within it, I must say this. As important as the law may be, you would be foolish to contemplate such a thought when an assault on your person is imminent. To think of such things will, without doubt, cause indecision which begets defeat. One second of indecision can mean the difference between defending yourself successfully and getting battered/raped/robbed. 'Better to be judged by twelve, than carried by six'.

Talk to any policeman or read any text on law and from out of the maelstrom of labyrinthian paragraphs and sub-paragraphs swims, again and again one word, 'reasonable'. An assault upon a person who is attacking or even about to attack you must show 'reasonable' force, if it is to be deemed as lawful. The dictioned word states:- 'In accordance with reason. Not extreme or excessive'. Section 3, Criminal Law Act 1967 states:- 'A person may use such force as is 'reasonable' in the circumstances, in the prevention of crime'.

In actuality, 'reasonable' force is dictated by the attacker/potential attacker. Even a serious wounding upon an adversary may be excusable if it is occasioned reasonably in the circumstances, and all the more justifiable in court, (though not essential), if the person claiming self-defence demonstrates that at the time of the assault/attempted assault, he did not want to fight. As coincidence would have it, this ties in nicely with my theories, as stated in Chapter 7 - 'Line-ups', on verbal, mental disarmament, i.e. telling your antagonist that you do not want to fight in order to mentally disarm him before you strike. Even the pre-emptive strike is tolerated in law, if the person claiming self-defence can again show that he was in imminent danger of assault and so attacked pre-emptively to stop the said assault. This may be demonstrated in law by the person claiming self-defence telling the police or courts, (if applicable), for example, that the antagonist shouted profanities at him and then moved aggressively toward him, forcing him to attack first. Again it helps if you can demonstrate that at the time you did not want to fight. Of course, the pre-emptive strike must be justified. If, for instance, your antagonist/potential antagonist had his hands in his pockets at the time of your pre-emptive strike, your actions would, no doubt, be seen as unlawful. Or if you stepped forward to deliver your pre-emptive strike, it may also be strewn as unlawful, because you moved toward him rather than he toward you. If you knock the person to the ground using reasonable force, to all intents and purposes, a further strike to the said person would be classed as unreasonable force, and therefore, unlawful, this also ties in nicely with my recommendation to 'hit and run'.

The use of incidental weapons, (as detailed in Chapter 4 - 'Attacking Tools'), may also be excusable in the law if the former criteria of 'reasonable force' is maintained. A 9st woman, for instance, being dragged unsolicitously into bushes by a 15st man who she stabs in the jugular with a pair of scissors, killing him, would very likely be dealt with leniently by any court in the land, though it is likely that she would have to demonstrate that the implied weapon was incidental, and therefore, not unlawful. Attacks with such weapons as knuckle dusters, flick knives and the like, even in defence, would in most cases be seen as unreasonable, and therefore, unlawful.

In brief and to sum up, the law states, in the case of self-defence of property or of another, (Butterworth - Police Law), self-defence and the defence of property or of another are common law defences. However, a person who acts in defence of himself, or another, or of property, is invariably acting in the prevention of crime in which case he also has the defence under the Criminal Law Act 1967, Section 3. For practical purposes, the terms of both the common law and the statutory defences are identical in their requirements.

The issue of self-defence as an excuse for a non-fatal offence against the person has been summarised extremely well by the court of appeal. The court said that it was both good law and good sense that a person who is attacked may defend himself, but that in doing so, he may only do what is reasonably necessary. The test of whether or not the force is reasonable is an objective one, but it is assessed on the facts as the person concerned believed them to be. It is also important, but not essential, that a person claiming self-defence demonstrated that he did not want to fight.

The law on defence of property or of another, is essentially the same as in self-defence, the essential question being 'was the force used reasonable in the circumstances?' Defence of property does not entitle the owner of property to use force against persons who trespass upon his land without offering force. In such a case the trespasser must be requested to leave before there is any hostile touching. If the trespasser is 'handled' it must amount to no more that is necessary to remove him from the property. If a trespasser offers force, then it may be met by whatever force is necessary to overcome it and remove him. If the owner of the land (house), is severely attacked, even a serious wounding may be excusable if it was occasioned reasonable in the circumstances, but it is always open to the other party to allege that the degree of force was excessive. For the avoidance of doubt, it must be stated that the mere fact that a person, who has used force against another was provoked to lose self-control, (as opposed to acting in self-defence, etc), is no excuse. Of course, if a person who has used provocative words or conduct then makes some immediately threatening move toward the person to whom his words or conduct are directed, he has carried out an assault, and reasonable resistance to it would amount to self-defence. If no more than provocation is involved, this is relevant in relation to the penalty which the court may award.

Again, I must re-emphasise that too much regard to 'how you stand within the law' could prove detrimental. The time to think about such things is afterwards when (if), the Police become involved. Basically, if you pre-emptively attack an attacker and then make your getaway, which is what I recommend, you should be safe in the eyes of the law.

As a final note:- The law differs from country to country, though most recognise the right to 'defend yourself'. The foregoing chapter should be used as a rule of thumb and not as actual fact. For more details contact your local Police station.

CHAPTER 26

EXTRA CURRICULUM

First and foremost, if you haven't already, join a self-defence club. There is no finer way to prepare yourself for self-defence than to join a club specialising in it. Always be careful to check out the instructors credentials, ensure that he is a bona fide instructor, and that his intentions are honourable. Most martial arts, boxing and wrestling are also worthy of your attention and may help markedly in your search for confidence and ability. Many, almost all in fact, sports that may not be directly relative to self-defence can help in the fitness side of things and also in sharpening up your reflexes, such as squash, badminton, running, etc Almost anything cardiovascular will be a good supplement.

Jogging. A great additive.

Weight training will develop strength and stamina which are both helpful in the execution of effective self-defence. Lifting weights can also be a great confidence builder, and confident people are not readily picked as targets for attacks.

Vigilance is an imperative that should, every day, be adhered to. Every time you leave the house, remind yourself that today could be the day. Practice vigilance when you get in and out of your car, when you go to work, when you return home, when you go out at night. I don't want you to become paranoid, just vigilant.

EPILOGUE

In the foregoing chapters we have explored self-defence in its entirety. If the preventative methods therein are conscientiously adhered to, you will undoubtedly reduce not only the chances of victimisation, but also the chances of failing to defend yourself should a situation arise.

Mastery of the techniques prescribed is not necessary, though competence surely is. It is not enough to look at the pictures, read the text and expect competence to automatically come. You must practice, rehearse and act out scenarios. Do not just practice them as perfunctory acts, visualise and make it real, put your mind into practice and make believe you are there. If your chosen partners for practice are giggly and silly, lose them, get yourself partners who want to practice seriously. Make self-defence an every day part of your life, like eating and drinking. Involve your family, children, spouses and remember, you don't have to be a victim, 'Fight Back'.

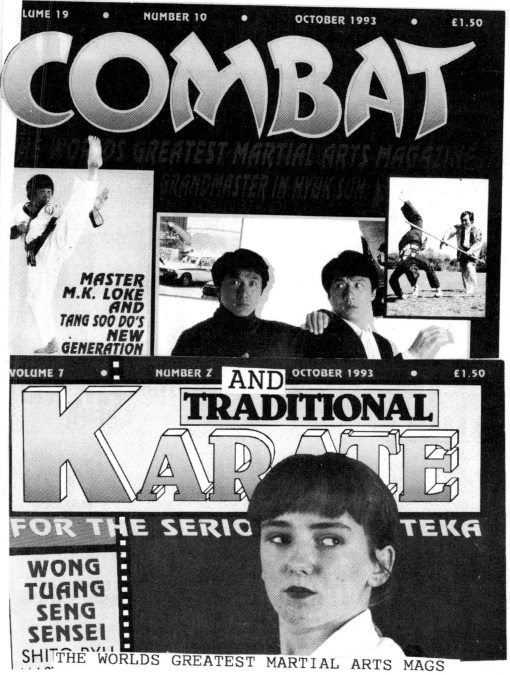

CENTRAL ENGLAND  KARATE ASSOCIATION

KARATE

COMPETITION KARATE

THE PAVEMENT ARENA

CHIEF INSTRUCTORS.
IAN McCRANOR (FOUNDER)
GEOFF THOMPSON

EKGB

TRADITIONAL KARATE

.Squad Training
.Trips Abroad
.Regional Courses etc

CENTRAL ENGLAND
KARATE ASSOCIATION

FOR INSTRUCTORS INFORMATION
CONTACT

19 Glebe Farm Grove, Bridgeacre Gardens, Spring
Valley, Coventry, CV3 2NE. Telephone: (0203) 443253

THE BRITISH COMBAT ASSOCIATION
THE ONLY ASSOCIATION DEDICATED TO SELF DEFENCE

Two of Britain's foremost Self Defence Instructors, Geoff Thompson and Peter Consterdine, have joined forces to form an Association which will promote the activities of Martial Artists pursuing the more practical aspects of their systems.

If you teach predominantly Self Defence or practical Martial Arts, then consider the following:

- *Are you fed up with the politics of large Association?*
- *Are you fully supported by the traditional groups?*
- *Are you prevented from seeking a wider range of instruction?*
- *Do you find it difficult to make your views felt? Is getting publicity for your group difficult?*
- *Are you and your junior instructors covered for liability insurance?*

- *Do you lack a regular flow of information on practical Martial Arts?*
- *Would you like to become a recognised Self Protection Instructor on a prestigious Register?*
- *Do you need assistance in promoting your Self Protection Course?*
- *Are you looking for Bodyguard and Small Arms Training?*

In the **British Combat Association**, together with its associated **Combat School and Self Protection Register**, we feel we have the answers. We can provide recognition, regular specialist training, gradings, insurance cover and a forum for your views. Your Club or Group will be actively promoted and publicised and the Association will, through a comprehensive syllabus and instructor assessment, professionalise the teaching of Self Protection.

The Register of Self Protection Instructors will become the prestigious reference point for people seeking professional teachers of Self Defence.

For an information pack send a large SAE to:-

The British Combat Association
Chel Centre
26 Roundhay Road
Leeds
LS7 1AB

Tel: 0532 429686 (Daytime office) or
Geoff Thompson on 0203 361741 or
Peter Consterdine on 0831 576509

In association with:-
The British Combat School & The Association & Register of Self Protection Instructors